DICKENS IN SEARCH OF HIMSELF

Dickens in Search of Himself

Recurrent Themes and Characters in the Work of Charles Dickens

Gwen Watkins

BARNES & NOBLE BOOKS
TOTOWA, NEW JERSEY

First published in Great Britain 1987 by
The Macmillan Press Ltd

First published in the USA 1986 by
BARNES & NOBLE BOOKS
81 ADAMS DRIVE
TOTOWA, NEW JERSEY 07512

ISBN 0-389-20643-1

Phototypeset in 11/12pt Palatino by
STYLESET LIMITED
Warminster, Wiltshire

Printed in Hong Kong

ISBN 0-389-20643-1

Library of Congress Cataloging-in-Publication Data
Watkins, Gwen.
Dickens in search of himself
Bibliography: p.
Includes index.
1. Dickens, Charles, 1812-1870—Criticism and
interpretation.   2. Self in literature.   3. Characters
and characteristics in literature.   I. Title.
PR4592.S38W38 1987   823'.8   86-10871
ISBN 0-389-20643-1

For My Children

Contents

The reader will see how impossible it is to say that the author is fully expressed in any speech, character or single work of his. One must first put all these together and relate them to a great synthesis of all the work, which will be found to possess a unity of its own, to which every separate work is ultimately related.

Dorothy L. Sayers, *The Mind of the Maker*

'Our whole life, Travellers,' said I, 'is a story more or less intelligible,—generally less; but we shall read it by a clearer light when it is ended. I, for one, am so divided this night between fact and fiction, that I scarce know which is which. . .'

Charles Dickens, *The Seven Poor Travellers*

Criticism does not exist to say about authors the things that they knew themselves. It exists to say the things about them that they did not know themselves.

G. K. Chesterton, Introduction to
The Old Curiosity Shop (Everyman Edition)

Introduction

In his essay on Edmund Spenser C. S. Lewis distinguishes between two different types of writer. Donne, he points out, 'wrote from his vivid consciousness of his own situation at a particular moment. He knew what he was putting into his poem, and we cannot get out of it more than he knew he was putting in. But Spenser, with his conscious mind, knew only the least part of what he was doing, and we are never sure that we have got to the end of his significance. The water is very clear, but we cannot see to the bottom.'[1]

Dickens is a writer of the second kind, whose significance is, in certain areas, inexhaustible. There are times when he knows exactly what he is doing – in most of the comic scenes, and in the great set pieces, such as Carker's ride from Dijon or the *Copperfield* storm scene – and exults in his own genius. No matter how often we read these, we cannot get from them more than he consciously put in, though that may be a great deal. But there are certain characters, certain themes, in which we constantly perceive fresh significance, new layers of meaning which open to reveal deeper meanings yet.

Sometimes the two kinds of writing collide, causing strange shifts in tone and emphasis often amounting to absolute contradiction, as though Dostoyevsky and P. G. Wodehouse were to collaborate. Dickens' two worlds are sometimes as widely separated as the worlds of Raskolnikov and Jeeves, and yet, because of his monstrous genius, we rarely question this. If any other author were so often to dislocate the levels of sensibility in this way, he would cause such a profound sense of unease in his readers that he would soon cease to be read at all. To change one's 'world' in mid-story is the novelist's deadliest sin; and yet (if like Chesterton we regard Dickens' whole *œuvre* as one long story) our greatest novelist does it constantly.

For instance, Tiny Tim 'hoped the people saw him in church, because he was a cripple, and it might be pleasant to them to remember upon Christmas Day, who made beggars walk ... '. Dickens is evidently quite unconscious that this manipulatory self-pity will later grow into Silas Wegg's frank exploitation of his disability, and the fact that Tim is a cripple is presented as a

tragic situation, while Wegg's amputated limb is a comic appur-
tenance in itself: ' . . . and I tell you openly I should *not* like . . . to
be what I may call dispersed . . . but should wish to collect
myself like a genteel person'.

Again, Mrs Gamp lives on the edge of that abyss which waited
for all the Victorian poor; she is only a little, and perhaps tem-
porarily, more secure than Jenny, the brickmaker's wife in *Bleak
House*, but the death of Jenny's child is tragedy while Mrs
Gamp's losses are material for comedy: ' "My own", I says, "has
fallen out of three-pair backs, and had damp doorsteps settled
on their lungs, and one was turned up smilin' in a bedstead,
unbeknown." ' The world of Mr F's Aunt is not the world of
Arthur Clennam; in her presence the man 'with an empty place
in his heart that he has never known the meaning of' becomes
merely the straight man in a comedy duo, because love and the
hunger for it do not exist in her world.

Dickens moves in and out of his two worlds with a total
unconsciousness that there is any difference between them,
because they are both equally real to him. Yet even readers who
dislike Dickens seldom or never refer to this as a reason for their
dislike; they speak of his one-dimensional characters or his sentimentality, but offer no investigation into the problem of why,
with such gross defects, he should still be regarded as one of our
greatest novelists. A few critics have commented on this
schizoid aspect of Dickens, though usually with a limited
application. Philip Collins, in his book on Dickens' attitudes to
education and crime, has shown how impossible it is to trace
any consistent line of reasoning on these subjects.[2] The same
man who makes Will Fern plead 'Give us kinder laws to bring us
back when we're a-going wrong; and don't set gaol, gaol, gaol,
afore us everywhere we turn' is the man who later says, 'Let us
have no Pet Prisoning, vain glorifying, strong soup and roasted
meats, but hard work, and one unchanging and uncompromis-
ing dietary of bread and water, well or ill'; and later still, 'I would
have his [the Ruffian's] back scarified often and deep.'

It is impossible to take Dickens seriously as a critic of social
conditions, since he has no consistent attitude to any social
question. Attempts to do so have led many critics, sincere
admirers of Dickens, into a jungle of misinterpretation and, at
worst, misreadings of what he is actually saying. Even his much-
praised sympathy for the poor shows itself only when the poor

are humble and respectful. He pities the plight of the children of the poor, condemned from their birth to a life of crime: 'Then we shall gather grapes from thorns, and figs from thistles; when fields of grain shall spring from the offal in the by-ways of our own wicked cities . . . then we may look for natural humanity and find it growing from such seed.' Yet when these children have grown to what they could not help being, he blames society no longer. 'I demand', he says, 'to have the Ruffian kept out of my way, and out of the way of all decent people' by 'a sentence of perpetual imprisonment'. In *A Christmas Carol* and in many of his journalistic pieces he puts forward the idea that education offers the only means of escape from their hopeless future for these children; yet in one of his last books Bradley Headstone, a pauper child who has been offered precisely this form of escape to a respectable life, ends with his career in ruins, a murderer and suicide. 'It is a leading characteristic of Dickens' mind', says John Carey, 'that he is able to see almost everything from two opposed points of view.'[3] He rightly draws attention to the split in Dickens' imagination, but confines his study mainly to an examination of the imagery of the novels and makes no attempt to explain or investigate the reason for this split. In my view it would be truer to say that there were actually two personalities in Dickens, the conscious and the unconscious self. This explains why both his 'worlds' were real to him; it explains Forster's statement that the books he wrote were never the books he planned – the conscious mind would project, the unconscious would take over. Forster, his lifelong friend and first biographer, perceived more than he fully understood about Dickens' relationship to his works.

'Men are enslaved by the forgotten, not the remembered, past.' It is the forgotten past, the wound inflicted on the infant psyche before the dawn of conscious memory, that forms Dickens' unconscious self. I believe that the recurrent types and themes that increasingly obsessed him from *Dombey* onwards rose from this self, and that he was continually impelled to examine and to explore them. Psycho-analysis attempts to draw these 'forgotten memories' from the unconscious into the conscious mind, and it seems to me that this is exactly what Dickens, without knowing it, is trying to do when he uses certain themes and certain character types. He lived too early to have any knowledge of the techniques of analysis, and had no way of interpreting the 'material' his unconscious mind presented to him; nevertheless, he does seem to have 'worked through' some of this material in very much the way an analyst would have tried to do, and by this means both to have come to terms with some of his psychological difficulties and to have opened the way to the search for deeper aspects of the self.

'I am, to myself, an unintelligible book, with the earlier chapters all torn out and thrown away,' says Barbox Brothers, the man who is running away from his own birthday. It is in an effort to show how Dickens himself provides material which may help to reconstruct those 'earlier chapters' that I have attempted to examine those themes which recur often enough to make us sure that they hold some special significance for their creator. For as Forster says, 'His literary work was so intensely one with his nature that he is not separable from it, and the man and his method throw a singular light on each other.'[4]

To uncover the roots of personality is never easy, even for the analyst whose patient is willing to help in the excavating. In doing it at second hand, and at a distance of time, one can only make conjectures about the material that is presented for analysis. We have some facts about Dickens' life, and we have a vast mass of autobiographical material in his writings; from these we can also select any other material that we think relevant. But this selection, the deductions we make from it and the interpretation we put upon it must depend to a great extent upon a personal viewpoint. 'Sometimes one conjectures right, and sometimes one conjectures wrong,' says Mr Frank Churchill in *Emma*. I believe that I may have conjectured right, for this reason. I have been reading Dickens all my life and soon became aware, as any one who reads him with passion and close attention must, that he was saying something else besides what he appeared to be saying and that this 'secret prose', as Graham Greene calls it, was of immense importance. I came to realise that the themes and characters which recurred were at the root of this sense of secondary life, but I knew very little about analytical techniques – nor, indeed, had I any knowledge of psychiatry in general, so that I could not advance in the understanding of what it was that Dickens was saying.

Then it became necessary, for reasons unconnected with my interest in Dickens, that I should study the phenomenon of early emotional deprivation and its consequences, in theory and in practice. I found that the themes that obsessed many people who had suffered from the lack of parental love were the same themes that recur so constantly in Dickens' work. When I read Dickens again, piece after piece of the jigsaw dropped into place of its own accord. But it was the writings that had interested me first. If things had happened the other way round, if I had first been interested in the techniques of analysis and had read Dickens to find interesting or relevant material, I should have been far less confident about my present thesis.

Even Dickensians who are not particularly sympathetic to psycho-analytical processes may, I think, admit that an interpretation of this kind does throw some light on what have hitherto been rather shady bits of Dickens. Incidents that may seem perfectly appalling mistakes as parts of the plot of a novel are seen to be inevitable to the perfect psychological truth of the unconscious mind. Little Nell is not merely an attempt to cash in on national sentimentality: she *must* die, as the true self of a child exploited – however lovingly – by the adults who should care for it must die. Dora's pathetic request to Agnes that only she should take Dora's place may have sickened critics from Chesterton onwards, but it is absolutely faithful to the needs of the unconscious: only Agnes, the 'good' mother-figure, *can* fill the 'vacant place' left by Dora's prototype, the inadequate mother.

Things that seem on a rational level to be without importance are seen on this other level to be full of significance. Arthur Clennam at the beginning of *Little Dorrit* feels that he must discover, and make restitution for, some secret crime of his father's, over whose secrecy hangs an oppressive air that taints his birthplace. The later plot reveals the crime to be his stepmother's, so that the marvellous description of Arthur's feeling that the whole city conceals, and yet is appalled at, the hidden crime would seem to be a mere dead end. But the real unconscious theme of the book is Arthur's guilt at his own existence, which has brought about the blight of his parents' and his stepmother's lives. The real crime has been his father's, in bringing Arthur to life.

Whatever is true, is true on many levels. To see Dickens as telling us what only the unconscious mind can know about the growth of the self is not to say that we must see him only in that way: we need lose nothing of all the other ways in which he can be read. But this interpretation has cast a flood of new light on his work for me, and I hope it may do so for others.

1

I Want to Escape from Myself

Only a unified personality, says Jung, 'can experience life; an occurrence split up into partial aspects, though it likewise call itself a human being, cannot do so'.

Every baby is born psychotic: that is, it has no appropriate perception of space or time, no consciousness of cause and effect, a total disregard for any needs but its own and no ability to satisfy those needs; it relies on other people for its survival and yet it shows them no consideration, much less gratitude, nor can it understand that they have needs and rights of their own. The baby is in fact neither able to live by itself nor, as yet, to adjust itself to the needs of a society able to support it. It is insane.

We are all born insant. Research by biologists, anthropologists, psychologists, psychiatrists, philologists, educationalists and many others has shown how we gradually attain a measure of sanity: that is, we learn how to live with ourselves and with others, and how to interpret the messages of our senses so that they fall into patterns which give our experience meaning. We have all the equipment for sanity when we are born (unless we are brain-damaged or genetically imperfect) but we must be taught by others how to use it. A baby who is wrongly or poorly taught may be unable to make sense of his world, and may remain permanently undeveloped in some areas of his personality.

Recent work by psychiatrists such as Jules Henry, Karen Horney, Bruno Bettelheim and R. D. Laing has given us a much deeper insight into such disturbances of the psyche. All these psychiatrists use differing terms for what they feel to be at the root of the disturbance: they call it alienation from self, identity loss, identity absence or ego failure, but what they mean is that the child's true self has never become unified – that, as Jung puts it, he remains 'split up into partial aspects'. This may

7

happen for many reasons. The child's parents may not want him, so that he is never given a sense of his own value; perhaps they love him only as extensions of themselves, so that he has to live their life, not his own; perhaps they themselves were so deprived of love that they have nothing but hostility to give him. Only a mature and stable love can give the new-born psyche the nourishment it needs to grow and become whole. Babies need continual repeated experiences in which pleasure and satisfaction outweigh anxiety and deprivation, in order to make patterns of these experiences which will teach them that their life is worth living and – even more important – that they are loved and accepted by those around them. If the patterns they make do not teach them this, they may become 'autistic': that is, they may make patterns of their own, unintelligible to others, and reject the experience of a world they find too harsh to endure.

Love will always respect the rights of another person, chief among them the right to be himself, and will value the uniqueness of that self. Emily Brontë was strong enough to write:

> Often rebuked, yet always back returning
> To those first feelings that were born with me[1]

but in few children is the young self so developed that it can sustain its 'first feelings' against the disapproval, perhaps the condemnation, of those it loves and needs. These feelings are what the child is, they are his very self, what he has brought into the world and what he has to give it; but if they are not accepted and valued he feels that they must be in some way 'bad' or 'wrong'. So what can he do? He may be so convinced that his elders are right that he becomes 'bad' in order to prove them so; or he may find the lack of love so intolerable that unconsciously he decides to destroy his 'bad' self and create a new self that will be loved and accepted.

In describing this process, even writers of psychological textbooks seem to need the language of tragedy or myth, as though in no other way could they speak of the death of the psyche. Jules Henry writes: 'Whence comes this immense sense of nothingness? Obviously out of having had something destroyed. A child was born, and cherished for a brief while ... And then the thing was crushed. But it was not obliterated: there was a distant memory of something that had been or almost had been. And this memory, so dangerous ... because it ... fills the soul with bursting rage . . . this memory is the headstone of that being who now stands before us, the cemetery of himself, yet visiting on those around him the persecuting phantom of his mutilated soul.'[2]

It seems obvious enough that, as Jules Henry says, identity loss is always rooted in the past. Bruno Bettelheim goes even further in suggesting that for those who suffer from such unresolved conflicts with themselves, since the source of these conflicts is in the past, that past may be experienced as though it were still present. In describing one of his autistic patients, he stresses that her life was so dominated by past experience that she was unable to believe that any event, however trivial, could ever be over and done with: 'That an experience is truly behind us requires the feeling that important past events can no longer shape the present for us . . . nothing was ever truly past for her. Hence the phenomenal memory of such children.'[3]

This preoccupation with the past may be the reason why autistic or schizophrenic children feel that 'concern for the preservation of sameness' observed by Erikson and Kanner. Only the past is real for them and therefore, if a semblance of reality is to be preserved, objects must remain exactly as they always have been. Bettelheim however advances another possible theory: that since the schizoid self has no permanency, the objects around it must remain unchanged, or the self may disintegrate or may even flow into the objects, which thus become of even greater importance since they actually contain the self. An obsessive preoccupation with the past may produce great intensity of vision, since the past has none of the blurred edges or faintness of distance because it is no more distant than the present. The schizoid self may even produce aural or visual hallucinations: voices may be heard or appearances seen as though they actually existed in the outside world.

The child who builds himself a second self to gain love and approval needs immense will-power to do so and to keep the true self from breaking through. A psychologist describes a patient who displayed the most rigid will to organise her life successfully until a breakdown at the age of forty: 'So what we see in our patient is a lonely pathetic infant, overcome with longing for what she never had. It seems clear that the great stress of "will-power" was a frantic reaction-formation, a desperate intention to compensate for her unfulfilled infantile needs, a strategy of living on, despite those early painful longings.' But the true self is always trying to break through, the infantile longings cannot be suppressed, and so the sufferer will be rent by powerful emotions that he does not understand and cannot control. The whole process is very exactly described by an anonymous patient of Karen Horney's, and we see that he too is compelled to use metaphors of crime and violence in telling what has happened to him:

> How is it possible to lose a self? The treachery, unknown and unthinkable, begins with our secret psychic death in childhood – if and when we are not loved and are cut off from our spontaneous wishes ... It is a perfect double crime ... not just the simple murder of a psyche, that might be written off [but] the tiny self also gradually and unwittingly takes part. He has not been accepted for himself as he is. Oh, they 'love' him, but they want him or force him or expect him to be different. Therefore he *must* be unacceptable. He himself learns to believe it and at last even takes it for granted. He has truly given himself up. No matter now whether he clings, rebels or withdraws – his behaviour, his performance, is all that matters. His centre of gravity is in 'them', not in him-self ... And the whole thing is entirely plausible, automatic and anonymous. This is the perfect paradox. Everything looks normal, no crime was intended, there is no corpse, no guilt. All we can see is the sun rising and setting as usual. But what has happened? He has been rejected, not only by them, but by himself. (He is actually without a self.) But alas, he is not dead. Life goes on, and so must he ... All unknowingly, he sets about to create and maintain a pseudo-self. But this is expediency – a self without wishes. This one shall be loved (or feared) where he is despised, strong where he is weak ... This necessity is not life – not his life; it is a defence mechanism against death. From now on, he will be torn apart by compulsive (unconscious) needs ... every motion and every instant cancelling out his being, his integrity; and all the while he is disguised as a normal person, and expected to behave like one.[4]

Most of our information about his childhood comes from Dickens himself. The prevailing tone of his own accounts of his childhood is, in spite of appearances to the contrary, one of anxiety and guilt. Many critics have felt that the blacking-factory episode was the great traumatic incident of his life from which all his later emotional difficulties proceeded. I do not see how this can be so. Children survive – perhaps with pain, but without permanent damage – such incidents as poverty, bereavement, social or other changes, war, invasion or physical suffering, if they know that they are supported and loved. It is impossible that a child truly cared for should be so neglected in times of difficulty as Dickens was by his parents. I do believe that the blacking-factory episode was of crucial importance in his life: it must have forced him to abandon any hope of help from those who should have been his guardians. Henceforth his childhood was dead and he had no parents. The knowledge must have remained dormant through the easier times that followed, but its result was inevitable. By the end of his adolescence he had begun to build that formidable shell of will-power and resolution which was to protect the desolate child within and to wring a recognition that he *was* worthy of love, not only from his parents, but from the whole world.

There is now no way to discover from actual historical evidence whether Dickens was the child of a mother herself so burdened with regressive infantile insecurities that she was unable to give her son the support he needed; nor can we know whether he was in fact forced to deny his true self and to create another. But if these things did happen to him, we should expect to find that some themes in his work dealt with these powerful unconscious motivations. I hope to prove that the major recurrent themes in Dickens' work do show a preoccupation with maternal deprivation, the split self, the destruction of the second self and the rebirth of the true self, but first it will be necessary to examine some facts about Dickens' life as they seem to me to be relevant to this question.

Many of Dickens' contemporaries had an acute perception of the two selves in the one person. Forster wrote of him:

What it was that in society made him often uneasy, shrinking, and over-sensitive, he knew; but all the danger he ran in bearing down and overmastering the feeling, he did not know. A too great confidence in himself, a sense that everything was possible to the will that would make it so, laid occasionally upon him self-imposed burdens greater than might be borne by anyone with safety. In that direction, there was in him, at such times, something even hard and aggressive ... something that made his resolves insuperable, however hasty the opinions on which they had been formed ... When I have seen, strangely present, at such chance intervals, a stern and even cold isolation of self-reliance side by side with a susceptivity almost feminine and the most eager craving for sympathy, it has seemed to me as though his habitual impulses for everything kind and gentle had sunk, for the time, under a sudden hard and inexorable sense of what Fate had dealt to him in those early years.[5]

To his children he was both the beloved and indulgent father and the feared, harsh disciplinarian who became 'almost a madman' at the time of his separation from his wife. George Dolby, his secretary and tour manager, who knew him only for the last four years of his life and regarded him with the utmost reverence, yet said of him: 'In him side by side lurked the iron will of a demon and the tender pity of an angel.'[6]

This 'iron will', once his fame and position were assured, was often used to impose his own ideas upon his world. Disagreement he could tolerate sometimes, disapproval never. He simply broke off relations with anyone who disapproved of his actions. His long friendship with Angela Burdett Coutts withered because she did not wholly sympathise with his attitude to his wife at the time of their separation. That wife, who had borne him ten children and had shared his bed for twenty years, simply ceased to exist for him. He never saw her again and during the rest of his life wrote her only three very brief notes. 'A page in my life that once had writing on it is now blank,' he wrote;[7] but the writing must be erased not only for himself but for those who wished to remain his friends. Mark Lemon was a lifelong friend; Dickens wrote to him after the baby Dora's death, 'I have not forgotten (and never shall forget) who sat up with me one night when a little place in my house was left empty.'[8] But when Lemon refused to publish in *Punch* Dickens' statement about the break-up of his marriage, he became 'false' and 'faithless', and the Dickens children were forbidden ever to speak to 'Uncle Mark' again.

Other friends felt this need of his to impose his own views on those around him. Macready, another lifelong friend, wrote in his journal: '[Forster] told me that Dickens is so intensely fixed on his own opinions, that . . . as he refused to see criticisms of himself, this partial passion would grow upon him until it became an incurable evil.'[9] Edmund Yates, one of his young men, wrote: 'The opinions which he held, . . . his ideas of what should, or should not, be, were all settled by himself, not merely for himself, but for all those brought into connection with him, and it was never imagined they could be called in question.'[10] Mrs Lynn Linton said that he was 'nervous and arbitrary', and that 'he was of the kind to whom whims are laws, and self-control in contrary circumstances was simply an impossibility'.[11]

But it was not only on his friends that he sought to impose his own view of reality and to assert his power. He had gained his reputation largely through fiction extolling what Keats called 'the holiness of the heart's affections', and his heroes and heroines sought domestic happiness as their greatest good. Yet when his marriage broke up with the maximum of publicity and in a flurry of scandal – it was said that his sister-in-law was his mistress, that he was the lover of a young actress – the enormous tide of his popularity rolled on undiminished, although his actions at this time bordered on insanity. Indeed, he actually chose to court the greatest possible publicity by beginning his career as a reader in public at the very time of the separation – 'publicly to show himself, at stated times, as a public entertainer',[12] says Forster, with frigid disapproval.

Not long afterwards, while seeking a name for the successor to *Household Words*, he hit upon the title *Household Harmony* and could not at all understand why Forster should try so earnestly to dissuade him from using it. 'I am afraid we must not be too particular about the possibility of personal references and applications,'[13] he said lightly; and it is only too evident that the huge brouhaha caused by his separation from his wife had no longer any existence in his mind, though a short time before it had occupied him furiously to the exclusion of all other matters. No doubt if he had chosen to use the name *Household Harmony* his readers would have accepted it docilely.

Forster found himself in a dilemma when, in the *Life*, he had somehow to describe and account for this aspect of Dickens. He did not understand the relentless psychological necessities which drove his friend, and supposed that the dissatisfactions he could not hide were with outer rather than inner events. 'Not his genius only, but his whole nature, was too exclusively made up of sympathy for, and with, the real in its most intense form, to be sufficiently provided against failure in the realities around him,'[14] was the best that Forster could do; but that grandiose sentence can only mean that Dickens simply could not come to terms with any kind of life that it was possible for him to live.

Dickens had sometimes a clearer notion of his own difficulties: at least he knew that the pressures came from inside himself. He first remarked on the compulsions which were to tear him apart for the rest of his life when he was trying to make a start on *Dombey and Son*, in which he deals for the first time with the major theme of the child rejected by a parent. About this time he also began, but did not finish, an account of his own childhood. Forster says that he could not bear to finish it, but perhaps his conscious mind could not tell him enough: it may have been myth he needed, not fact. In 1848 Dickens began to complain of bodily and mental restlessness which interfered with his work. In a letter to Angela Burdett Coutts in 1845 he had complained that for three months he had been driven to wander round Italy: 'I have been constantly and incessantly on the wing, and have been so cold and so wet, and so muddy, ... and have led altogether such a wild, preposterous life – that I have not had the heart to write to you'.[15] How much of his life was passed in this disoriented way we do not know, nor how often he was compelled to roam about distractedly at the behest of his inner tormentor. He might be in the middle of a page, when 'it suddenly came into my head that I would get up and go to Calais. I don't know why; the moment I got there I should want to go somewhere else.'[16] He came to accept these compulsions as a part of his life: 'Such a torment ... takes hold of me, that it is like being *driven away*,' he wrote;[17] and again, 'I am the modern embodiment of the old Enchanters, whose Familiars tore them to pieces.'[18]

Dickens' passion for acting may have had its origin in a desire to get away from the self he had created (and perhaps too it was an unconscious desire to find his real self). 'I feel a loss of Oh I can't say what exquisite foolery, when I lose a chance of being someone not in the remotest degree like myself,' he wrote.[19] Forster apparently recognised this compulsive element when he said that the theatrical interludes 'expressed but the craving which still had possession of him to get by some means at some change that should make existence easier'.[20]

The Readings were an extension of his theatrical activities. It is significant that although they did not begin until 1858, Dickens first had the idea of doing something of the sort at the very time when he was trying, and failing, to make a start on *Dombey*. 'I was thinking the other day,' he wrote to Forster, 'that . . . a great deal of money might possibly be made (if it were not infra dig.) by having Readings of one's own books. It would be an *odd* thing. I think it would take immensely.'[21] Forster strongly opposed the idea, but it came up again at another period of disturbance. In 1857, at the end of a letter describing his sense of desolation at having missed 'the one happiness' in life and the 'miseries of older growth' threatening to close around him, Dickens asked: 'What do you think of my paying for Gadshill by reviving that old idea of some Readings for my books?' Almost immediately he dropped the financial motive to confess, 'I must do *something*, or I shall wear my heart away.'[22] Finally he began the Readings in the same month that his separation from his wife was being arranged.

What happened then was the fulfilment of a megalomaniac's fantasy. Dickens came into contact with an audience to whose presence and reactions he was alive with the acutest sensibility. He alone had devised and was presenting the performance they watched; he stood alone before them while he read, and he stood alone in their hearts. He, who had once been so helpless, so completely at the mercy of other people, now exercised immense power over thousands. He could make them laugh or cry uncontrollably; make them wait hours, or even days, for tickets to hear him read; once he prevented a panic by his imperturbability. 'We turned away hundreds upon hundreds of people', he wrote,[23] and later, 'A most tremendous hall here last night: something almost terrible in the cram',[24] and 'No one can imagine the scene of last Friday night at the embassy . . . a two-hours' storm of excitement and pleasure. They actually murmured and applauded right away into their carriages and down the street.'[25]

Perhaps his parents had not loved him as he needed to be loved; now he could get nightly demonstrations of love and approval from the whole world. It became his drug, and he would almost kill himself to get it. Lame, catarrhal, almost voice-less, so ill and exhausted towards the end that he had to have a guard near him to support him in case he should collapse, once on the platform he would give a performance of such magnificent vitality that his audiences would refuse to leave in the hope of another word from the Master.

His doctor and his friends thought that the Readings were killing him; perhaps they were, but they were also the drug that kept him alive. But it was never enough. Dr Daniel Casriel says of this situation, 'Actors don't trust the approval they get ... Going before an audience becomes in effect an addiction. It doesn't solve their neurosis; it feeds it. Each time they go before an audience it is like throwing another log on the fire of their anxiety. It fuels their anxiety, it doesn't cure it. Success never makes most actors secure.'

Dickens' preoccupation with the past is strongly in evidence in his writings: Angus Wilson indeed calls his obsession with childhood one of his two great defects. But was this the inability to have done with the past which Bettelheim sees as the mark of one who is searching for his own identity? Kathleen Tillotson appears to feel (though from a purely literary standpoint) that there is something abnormal about it, when she says that 'Dickens, while exceptionally aware of his past, is exceptionally unaware of his distance from it'. Dickens himself had some perception of the *recurrent* nature of past experience. He wrote to Forster in 1862:

> I must entreat you to pause for an instant, and go back to what you know of my childish days, and to ask yourself whether it is natural that something of the character formed in me then, and lost under happier circumstances, should have re-appeared in the last five years. The never-to-be-forgotten misery of that old time, bred a certain shrinking sensitiveness in a certain ill-clad ill-fed child, that I have found come back in the never-to-be-forgotten misery of this later time.[26]

Only two major critics of Dickens' own time seem to have caught the note of abnormality to which most of his contemporaries were deaf. Henri Taine saw that Dickens' imagination possessed depth but not breadth, and that this very intensity caused him to give too great an emphasis to the unchanging rather than the changing quality of personality. Taine may not have realised that these sharp edges, this vividness, came from an inner preoccupation with the past, but he did realise that the effects they produced were 'in the style of sickness rather than of health'.[27] He also noticed Dickens' sense of inanimate objects as symbolic – 'imaginary objects take the precision of real ones'[28] – and felt his power to draw his readers into his own fantasies.

G. H. Lewes carried this point further. He thought that Dickens actually had hallucinations, 'of which the revived impressions to him had the vividness of sensations, and the images his mind created in explanation of them had the coercive force of realities'. 'What seems preposterous, impossible to us,' says Lewes, 'seemed to him simple fact of observation. . . . So definite and insistent was the image, that even while knowing it was false we could not help, for a moment, being affected, as it were, by his hallucination.'[29] 'I hope my readers will be able to understand that,' says Forster patronisingly.[30] Perhaps most Victorian readers did not understand; but Lewes appears to be giving, in the language of his time, a pretty good account of how the unconscious mind does in fact work and of its effect on those brought into contact with it.

To listen to these messages from the inner self, to create images from them in his writing, and to engage in ceaseless activity were Dickens' only means of relief from internal pressures which built up relentlessly. After *Dombey* his life becomes more and more a record of restlessness, frustration, depression and stress. 'I seem to be always looking for something I have not found in life, but may possibly come to a few thousand years hence, in some other part of some other system. God knows', he wrote despairingly to Mary Boyle in 1852.[31] And later, to Forster, 'However strange it is to be never at rest, and never satisfied, and ever trying after something that is never reached . . . how clear it is that it must be, and that one is driven by an irresistible might until the journey is worked out.'[32] And later still, 'Too late to say, put the curb on . . . the wrong man to say it to. I have now no relief but in action. I am become incapable of rest. I am quite confident that I should rust, break and die, if I spared myself. Much better to die, doing. Restlessness, you will say. Whatever it is, it is always driving me, and I cannot help it.'[33]

'*It is always driving me, and I cannot help it.*' What could it be that was driving him but his own self, that self that he had helped to murder, that left an 'empty place in his heart that could never be filled'? That self did its best to help him by sending up to his imagination those themes that recur so constantly in his novels: the death of a child, the empty heart, the double self, the murder of the self. Almost certainly, Dickens was not aware of his own involvement with these themes, although he frequently reports experiencing exhausting emotional crises (such as are familiar to anyone undergoing psycho-analysis) when beginning or ending work on them.

G. K. Chesterton and Graham Greene are the only two critics who seem sensitive to this undercurrent running through all Dickens' work. Greene refers to 'the tone of Dickens' secret prose, that sense of a mind speaking to itself, with no one there to listen'.[34] And Chesterton has realised that many of the characters in the novels are archetypes, personal myths, when he says, 'It seems almost as if these grisly figures, Mrs Chadband and Mrs Clennam, Miss Havisham and Miss Flite, Nemo and Sally Brass, were keeping something back from the author as well as the reader . . .'.[35]

'Even now,' says Dickens, in the autobiographical fragment, 'famous and caressed and happy, I often forget in my dreams that . . . I am a man; and wander desolately back to that time of my life.'[36] Forster described him as 'master of everything that might seem to be attainable in life', but he lacked the one thing that Jung says is necessary for a true experience of life – a unified self. In his life and in his work Dickens was always to be in search of himself.

2

A Vacancy in my Heart

'I do not write resentfully or angrily; for I know how all these things have united together to make me what I am: but I never afterwards forgot, I never shall forget, I never can forget, that my mother was warm for my being sent back.'[1] It is strange that Dickens should, at the age of thirty-five, express such burning hostility (in spite of his denials it is clear that he *did* feel both anger and resentment) against his mother because of an incident which happened twenty years before, and yet express no such hostility against his father. If anyone was to be blamed for Charles' misery at that time, it must be John Dickens: his irresponsibility, perhaps even his dishonesty, had brought the family to circumstances where the earning by one child of six or seven shillings a week was a relief, and when he himself was released from the Marshalsea through the slow procedures of the Insolvency Act in May 1824, it seems not to have occurred to him to release his child ('quick, eager, delicate, and soon hurt, bodily or mentally'[2]) from a much more terrible servitude.

Dickens indicts both his parents as almost criminally thoughtless: 'My father and mother were quite satisfied. They could hardly have been more so if I had been twenty years of age, distinguished at a grammar-school, and going to Cambridge.'[3] Both appear to have been unconscious of the child as a child, and of his physical or emotional needs. Physically he was completely neglected (although he had not been a robust child, and still suffered from his 'old attacks of spasm' both at the factory and at his lodgings in Lant Street). He had to support himself on six or seven shillings a week.

> I suppose my lodging was paid for by my father. I certainly did not pay it myself; and I certainly had no other assistance whatever (the making of my clothes, I think, excepted), from Monday morning until Saturday night . . . I know that I tried, but ineffectually, not to anticipate my money, and to make it last the week through by putting it away in a drawer I had in

the counting-house, wrapped into six little parcels, each parcel containing the same amount, and labelled with a different day. I know that I have lounged about the streets, insufficiently and unsatisfactorily fed. I know that, but for the mercy of God, I might easily have been, for any care that was taken of me, a little robber or a vagabond.[4]

Both parents appear to have been equally unaware that a twelve-year-old child, cast out to live alone, could need anything more than clothes, a lodging, and a visit to the family once a week. But Dickens' own words still vibrate with the intensity of the pain he felt twenty-three years before.

No words can express the secret agony of my soul ... the deep remembrance of the sense I had of being utterly neglected and hopeless ... My whole nature was ... penetrated with grief and humiliation ... That I suffered in secret, and that I suffered exquisitely, no one ever knew but I. How much I suffered, it is ... utterly beyond my power to tell.[5]

He never did tell his parents, apparently, at that time or at any other time in his life; perhaps he felt that to have told them would have made no difference. The child was abandoned to his own desolation: 'No advice, no counsel, no encouragement, no consolation, no support, from anyone that I can call to mind, so help me God.'[6]

A good deal has been made of the elder Dickens' circumstances at this time, in extenuation of their treatment of Charles. Edgar Johnson says that 'in the self-absorbed grief of childhood, Charles hardly realised how frantic his parents were with anxiety, or what a relief even this provision for one of their children must be to them ... And there was reason enough to be frightened. There was no way in which he [John Dickens] could pay his debts ... He had been in the Navy Pay Office nineteen years, but a man who incurred the disgrace of insolvency could hardly hope to be retained there. In that case, income, pension possibilities, all hope, would vanish.'[7] This may be true, but in fact John Dickens was in receipt of his salary of £350 a year during the whole time when his son was left to support himself on six or seven shillings a week. A legacy of £450 from his aged mother, paid in June after his release, helped to pay some of his

debts; he still had hopes of his pension, since on his imprisonment he had sent the Pay Office a medical certificate of his unfit-
ness for duty; and for the time being he had returned to
work.

Dickens seems reluctant to accuse his father of anything but
thoughtlessness: 'in the ease of his temper and the straitness of
his means, he appeared to have utterly lost at this time the idea
of educating me at all, and to have utterly put from him the
notion that I had any claim upon him, in that regard, whatever'.[8]
But it is thoughtlessness of a very high order indeed which can
leave a twelve-year-old to the dangers, the difficulties and the
solitude of London for six days in every week. It is worth noting
that in all his distress Dickens never apparently thought of
appealing to his mother, or even of seeking sympathy from her,
as most children would do.

> On Sunday night I remonstrated with my father on this head,
> so pathetically and with so many tears, that his kind nature
> gave way. He began to think that it was not quite right. I
> believe he had never thought so before, or thought about
> it.[9]

The thoughtlessness, however monumental, which had caused
a child to suffer bitterly at last turned to kindness and rescued
him. His mother (who must have arranged his Camden Town
lodging, since his father had then been in prison for some
weeks) now tried to force him back into the factory. But the difference in his attitude towards his parents can only have been
brought to a head by these incidents: the attitudes themselves
must already have been strongly founded. It is obvious that
although both parents made use of him and neglected him,
there was some warmth and appreciation of his son in the
father, even if only intermittently and even if only appreciation
of an object useful or entertaining to himself, that made it
possible for Charles to come to terms with the bitterness and
pain he must have felt about his father's treatment of him. He
was to be wildly exasperated by his father's continuing financial
irresponsibility, to the point of publicly refusing to discharge his
father's debts and insisting that he leave the country. John
Dickens did not go abroad, and his quarterly allowance from
Charles continued to be paid. Charles wrote bitterly to a correspondent in 1841: 'Your father, like many I know, takes after the

birds, and forgets his children as soon as they can fly. But that's not the worst that can happen. I know some men who would be heartily glad, with reason, if their fathers would forget them altogether . . . '.[10] But in the writing of *David Copperfield* 'all that had been best in his father', says Forster, 'came more and more vividly back to its author's memory; as time wore on, nothing else was remembered; and five years before his own death, after using in one of his letters to me a phrase rather out of the common with him this was added: "I find this looks like my poor father, whom I regard as a better man the longer I live." '[11]

There was no such softening towards his mother. There are far fewer references to her in the autobiographical fragment, the letters or the journalism. It was his father who took him for walks, his father who proudly exhibited him to friends as a singer of comic songs, his father who provided the books which so nourished his imagination, his father who gave him the intoxicating idea that he might one day own Gadshill. We have the impression of a careless if genial personality, but we can gain no impression at all of his mother. Dickens told Forster that his mother had taught him the rudiments of English and Latin 'thoroughly well',[12] so that when he referred contemptuously to her plans for Mrs Dickens' Establishment, it was not her teaching abilities that he despised. Nor did he as a small child dislike the passion for gossip which he afterwards satirised in Mrs Nickleby: 'When I went to the Marshalsea of a night, I was always delighted to hear from my mother what she knew about the histories of the different debtors in the prison.'[13] Forster says mysteriously and without explanation that Dickens told him that 'his mother had been in the blacking warehouse many times; his father not more than once or twice.'[14] Was this another reason for the child's growing hostility to his mother? Was she a frequent and uncaring witness to his humiliation, whereas his father immediately put an end to it?

The references to her in his letters are of the slightest and most commonplace kind. Once he is moved to say, 'I do swear that I am sick at heart with both her and father too.'[15] Most psychologists think that the child must 'react in a fruitful way' with his mother (or mother-substitute) if his later emotional development is to be successful. The mother must make the child feel that *what he is*, his self, is valuable and worthy of respect, and that he is loved because this self is lovable. If the child is not loved in this way, he feels himself to be 'bad' (that is, not what his parents want); he will probably feel guilt at not being 'good', perhaps even guilt at being born, since he is so patently not what they want. He may tend to separate 'good' from 'bad' not only in himself but in others too.

All these themes occur in Dickens' work, as we shall see. But the mother will also, by what *she* is, give the child an unconscious expectation of what women will be in his adult life: if he sees women as cruel or rejecting, he will either be attracted to women who are so in reality, or will so manoeuvre by his own behaviour women who are not like this, that they will either genuinely reject him or seem to him to do so.

We have seen that Elizabeth Dickens was an uncaring and neglectful mother towards Charles when the family was in difficulties; Charles may well have felt himself actually rejected, since his sister Fanny was being educated by means of a scholarship at the Royal Academy of Music, while he himself was merely a household drudge. It seems to me very likely that Elizabeth Dickens was in fact always a poor mother, though as evidence for this we must take mainly Dickens' writings and the fact of his lack of affection for her in later years. If, as is generally thought, 'bad' mothers reflect towards their children the quality of their own mothering, it is interesting to note that Elizabeth Dickens was the second child of a mother married at sixteen who had eleven children in seventeen years, of whom the first five were born in six years. Elizabeth was born when her first sister was twelve months old, and the next child arrived fourteen months later. Until she was thirteen, when her father was appointed to a responsible position in the Navy Pay Office, the circumstances of the household were very moderate, so perhaps she too was a 'not-over-particularly-taken-care-of' child. (It is interesting to note, too, that she followed the pattern of her own upbringing in marrying a man like her father, irresponsible to the point of dishonesty in financial matters.)

Elizabeth married at the age of nineteen, and Charles too was the second child of a numerous family, born before his sister was eighteen months old; another child, to die in infancy, was conceived not long after his birth. The pictures of Mrs Jellyby's and Mrs Pocket's families, 'not growing up or being brought up, but . . . tumbling up', may ironically enough describe not only

Elizabeth Dickens' children, but also her mother's children. Dickens' own fanatical orderliness in adult life was a protest against his mother's slipshod and neglectful management.

But to react against an idea or a way of life is to be as strongly possessed by it as if it is held to and followed. The cold dislike which seems to have been Dickens' only emotion for his mother in adult life was a part of the second self or persona, but within the inner or true self – or the vacancy where that self should have been – there remained the rejected child seeking desperately either for the mother he had never had, or perhaps for that very early relationship with the mother, in the first few weeks after birth, which Jung thinks the origin of the myth of Paradise. 'The feature of over-estimation', he says, 'by which the loved one becomes the unique, the irreplaceable one, fits just as readily into the infantile set of ideas, for no one possesses more than one mother, and the relation to her rests on an experience which is assured beyond all doubt and can never be repeated.'

It is possible that in this sense Catherine Hogarth was a mere irrelevance in Dickens' life: it was the persona, the second self, who chose her, for motives of policy. Dickens wanted and could afford to get married; he married rather above him (as his father had done); he made a conscious, not an unconscious, choice. Maria Beadnell, as I shall show, reminded him of his mother: she had (in his terms) betrayed him as his mother had betrayed him, and therefore his deep emotional involvement with her had some hold upon him until the touch of reality, when he met her again in 1855, released him. Undoubtedly the reality of marriage with her would have dispelled in the same way his illusions of a lifelong love ('I never have loved and I never can love any human creature breathing but yourself'[16]). It is possible that even had she accepted him his feelings might have begun to change at once. Perhaps betrayal and loss were so strongly associated with his pattern of love that he needed them as much as he needed the love.

Certainly when he became infatuated with Christiana Weller, upon meeting her at a soirée of the Mechanics' Institution at Liverpool, he immediately associated her with a possible early death – merely, it would seem, because he had fallen in love with her and for no other reason. 'I cannot joke about Miss Weller,' he wrote, 'for she is too good; and interest in her (spiritual young creature that she is, and destined to an early death, I fear) has become a sentiment with me. Good God, what a madman I should seem, if the incredible feeling I have conceived for that girl should be made plain to anyone.'[17] She immediately took on the 'mythic' quality that the women who answered his unconscious needs must always hold for him: 'Hours of hers are years in the life of common women ... it is in such a face and such a spirit, as parts of its high nature, to do at once what less ethereal creatures must be long in doing.'[18] Her musical career 'should not be called her life but Death ... I could better bear her passing from my arms to Heaven, than I could endure that thought of coldly passing into the world again to see her no more.'[19]

There appears to have been no foundation for Dickens' passionate apprehension that Christiana was too 'young, beautiful and good' for this world: she seems to have been perfectly healthy, and she lived to marry T. J. Thompson and bear him two daughters, one of whom was to become Alice Meynell. Her fall from the role of the unattainable destroyed her power over Dickens.[20] 'She seems ... to have a devil of a whimpering, pouting temper',[21] he wrote when he met her again several years later; and to another correspondent, 'She is a mere spoiled child, I think, and doesn't turn out half as well as I expected.'[22]

If he could have married her, as he undoubtedly would have done had he been free to do so, her fate would have been no different from that of Catherine, though she was greatly superior to Catherine in intelligence and culture. But there was in Dickens a great deal of hostility towards women who attracted him. He needed to punish them either because they threatened the self-sufficient persona he had built up or because they reminded him of his mother, whom he could never sufficiently punish. The description of David's infatuation with Dora is probably a true picture of his own feeling for Maria Beadnell in one of its aspects, but the letters we have to her (admittedly after a supposed change in her feelings towards him) do not by any means express uncritical adoration. There is a good deal of resentment and self-justification in them.

Thank God! I can claim for myself and feel that I deserve the merit of having ever throughout our intercourse acted fairly, intelligibly and honourably. Under kindness and encouragement one day and a total change of conduct the next I have ever been the same ... I have never held out encouragement which I knew I never meant; I have never indirectly sanctioned hopes which I well knew I did not intend to fulfil ... I have borne more from you than I do believe any creature breathing ever bore from a woman before ... Destitute as I am of hope or comfort I have borne much and I dare say can bear more.[23]

His letters to Catherine before their marriage are often sharply critical of her, while allowing her no criticism of himself.

I owe a duty to myself as well as to you, and as I was wild enough to think that an engagement of even three weeks might pass without any such display as you have favoured me with twice already, I am the more strongly induced to discharge it ... the sudden and uncalled-for coldness ... such sullen and inflexible obstinacy ... If a *hasty* temper produce this strange behaviour, acknowledge it when I give you the opportunity. ... I hope ... you have no new complaints either *bodily* or *mental* ... if you would only determine to *shew* the same affection and kindness to me, when you felt disposed to be ill-tempered ... [24]

Perhaps he was hostile to most women, not only to those to whom he was attracted. There is no evidence that he was at any time in love with Georgina, and in any case she took care to make herself in every detail exactly what he wanted her to be. On the rare occasions when she failed in this she was given a sharp reproof.

About Dickens' relationship with Ellen Ternan we can only hazard guesses: if there is anything of her in Estella, Bella Wilfer and Rosa Bud, there is a good deal of evidence of his feeling for her in the tortured and ambivalent attitudes of Pip, John Harmon and Edwin Drood. She certainly did not become his mistress for some time after he first fell in love with her. Thomas Wright, that most mendacious of biographers, said that she told him that she was not at all in love with Dickens. If this was so, then he had again been betrayed and in some sort rejected. The inexorable pattern had repeated itself and he was too old and too tired to make any more attempts at breaking out of it.

If only the unattainable She could hold Dickens permanently it is not surprising that Mary Hogarth should have possessed him for so long. Death has many more overtones for the unconscious than for the conscious mind. The dead instantly become a part of the past; they are crystallised and enshrined, no part of the irritations and disillusions of every day. 'The lost paradises are the only true ones', says Gide, and Mary Hogarth, by moving into the past and becoming forever unattainable, had become the Eve (wife and mother) of Dickens' lost paradise. In addition, to the child mind Death is the great betrayal: the dead mother has rejected him once for all. So Mary managed to fit into the pattern of betrayal while yet remaining faultless. However it has not, I think, usually been noticed that it seems to have been her death alone that triggered off his passionate idealisation of her. 'I solemnly believe that so perfect a creature never breathed . . . She had not a fault', he wrote to Beard.[25] Forster says that by 'sweetness of nature even more than by graces of person Mary had made herself the ideal of his life',[26] but he must be relying on what Dickens himself had said, since Forster visited him for the first time only after Mary's death, when Dickens was in the first anguish of bereavement.

There is no doubt that Mary was a pretty and pleasant girl, and her brother-in-law probably found her more congenial company than the lethargic Kate, who had given birth to Charley only five months before and was again pregnant; but if he was in fact in love with her before her death he has left no recorded evidence of the fact, which is very unlike the usual behaviour when in love of one who was only too ready to bring his friends and even his public either directly or obliquely into the circle of his emotions. In the number of *Martin Chuzzlewit* immediately following the beginning of his infatuation for Christiana Weller he was impelled to bare his heart to his readers (having already been a good deal more explicit to Thompson, who was also in love with her) with deft references to both Mary and Christiana.

Somebody who is precious to you may die, and you may dream that you are in heaven with the departed spirit, and you may find it a sorrow to wake to one life on earth, which is no harder to be borne than when you fell asleep. . . . Are my words to be harsh and my looks to be sour, and is my heart to grow cold, because there has fallen in my way a good and beautiful creature, who, but for the selfish regret that I cannot call her my own, would, like all other good and beautiful creatures, make me happier and better!

But any such feelings that he had for Mary seem to have passed without record – his own or anyone else's. Wright indeed says that Catherine 'resented . . . being relegated to the background by Mary',[27] but Wright is a notoriously unreliable witness and can bring no evidence for his statement, nor for another assertion that before Mary's death Dickens was 'outrageously eulogistic' about her.[28] She was referred to by Robert Story as 'a beautiful and light-hearted girl', and by John Strong, City Chamberlain of Glasgow, as a 'sweet interesting creature'. In a letter to Catherine during their engagement Dickens says, 'Give my love to Mary and tell her I rely on her characteristic kind-heartedness, and good nature to accompany you . . . '.[29] He also gave Mary a copy of each number of *Pickwick* as it came out, inscribed 'most affy. Charles Dickens'. There is also no evidence that she lived with the young couple, as has been assumed by most biographers, from shortly after their marriage; references in Dickens' letters and one surviving letter of hers (curiously enough in a style not altogether unlike that of Flora Casby) seem to indicate that she did no more than pay frequent, and sometimes long, visits to them. Too much reliance, or perhaps too strong an interpretation, has been placed on Dickens' assertion after her death 'that from the day of our marriage the dear girl had been the grace and life of our home, our constant companion, and the sharer of all our little pleasures'.[30]

But immediately after her death his emotions were made public in a way that almost suggests that they originated in that death. To Ainsworth he wrote of 'the dear girl whom I loved, after my wife, more deeply and fervently than any one on earth'.[31] 'I have lost the dearest friend I ever had,' he wrote to Johns; 'Words cannot describe the pride I felt in her, and the devoted attachment I bore her.'[32] In every extant letter about her death, even in a formal note to Edward Chapman, he records the fact that she died 'in my arms'.[33] In the June issue of *Bentley's Miscellany* he referred to her as 'a dear young relative to whom he was most affectionately attached and whose society has been for a long time the chief solace of his labours' – which must have made rather painful reading for Catherine, as must his impassioned statements that Mary had been 'the grace and life of our home' and that 'the light and life of our happy circle is gone'. They had after all been married only thirteen months, but it is evident that Catherine had already ceased to be, if indeed he had ever thought her so, the centre of his emotional life. Some difficulties or disappointments, evidently of such a kind as to make Dickens realise that there could be no real affinity between them, had already arisen 'in the days . . . when Mary was born'.[34] By the second anniversary of their wedding the success of Dickens' 'second self', who was to bring him fame wealth and admiration, was assured; Boz was a household word, and the first number of *Nicholas Nickleby* had sold nearly 50 000 copies on the first day of its publication. More and more from this time on, the true self was to assert itself; the skeleton, imbued with fearful life, was to rattle incessantly at the cupboard doors.

With Mrs Nickleby we have the first exploration of the theme of the mother. Dickens is supposed to have hinted that the portrait was truthfully based on the character of his mother: 'Mrs Nickleby herself, sitting bodily before me in a solid chair, once asked me whether I really believed there ever was such a woman!'[35] It is a 'conscious' portrait, keeping within the Victorian convention that a mother, if not 'bad', *must* be good and *must* have no interest in anything but her children's welfare – and yet contriving to show Mrs Nickleby's selfish stupidity and her complete inability to see the facts of any situation while convinced that no one but herself can do so. If it is at all a true picture of Elizabeth Dickens, it is a fearful indictment.

Mrs Nickleby's chief and worst characteristic is her overriding concern for herself and lack of concern for others; she has in fact no real perception of other people. Did Elizabeth Dickens 'come to persuade herself that of all her . . . husband's creditors, she was the worst used and the most to be pitied'? Mrs Nickleby was 'at no time remarkable for the possession of a very clear understanding' and 'not the sort of person to be told anything in a hurry'. She 'talked incessantly, and did something now and then, but not often'; she was 'perfectly satisfied to be talking, and caring very little whether anybody listened or not'. She knows that in every case 'her conjecture could not fail to be the right

one', although her perception of other people and her interpretation of facts are so faulty that her conjectures are always,
and sometimes dangerously, wrong.

Mrs Nickleby, with 'a weak head and a vain one' but 'no evil
and little real selfishness', provides only a background of
comedy to her children's lives, although Nicholas is sometimes
'fretted almost beyond endurance'. And yet . . . she is perfectly
satisfied that her daughter shall marry for position: worse, she
betrays Kate into a close association with men whom even her
complacent stupidity should see for what they are. Her advice
has led to her husband's ruin and death; she would, if she could,
destroy the happiness of Tim Linkinwater and Miss La Creevy;
she has in her the seeds of Mrs Vardon, Mrs Skewton, Mrs
General, Mrs Sparsit – all the women who have no real
apprehension of the existence of love.But because she is a comic
figure, her creator need not take seriously either her potential
for harming others or the real harshness of such a portrait –
harsh because Mrs Nickleby has no good points at all. It is said of
her that she had loved her husband and 'had no greater share of
selfishness than is the usual lot of mortals', she is supposed to
picture 'with the brightness of a mother's fancy all the beauty
and grace of the poor girl who had struggled so cheerfully with
her new life of hardship and trial'; but in fact she sees no
hardships but her own and thinks of her family as mere adjuncts
to her own advantage: 'indeed, I don't know any use there
would be in having sons at all, unless people could put confidence in them'.

But after all Nicholas is an adult and his mother, however
stupid and selfish, cannot really harm him. A few months after
Dickens had written the autobiographical fragment, he began to
explore in *David Copperfield* the theme of the child exposed to a
mother's selfishness and stupidity, and this time it is a serious
confrontation – though not yet a direct one. Dickens is not yet
ready to face the possiblity that a mother simply *could* not love
the child enough to take care of it. When the small Copperfield
becomes what the small Dickens had been, his mother is dead;
but all the same it is she who has betrayed him into this ruin. Mrs
Copperfield is pretty and charming and helpless, and so we do
not realise – and Dickens is not prepared to admit – that she is
as insensitive and selfish as Mrs Nickleby. (Charm and helplessness, in fact, seem to have been Dickens' Loadstone Rock: Maria

Beadnell was charming and helpless; Christiana Weller was
charming and seemed helpless when he first met her; Mme de la
Rue was 'a most affectionate and excellent little woman'[36]
helpless in the grip of her hallucinations; Ellen Ternan was
small, fair-haired and charming, and if she was not helpless she
'had brains' and probably knew how to appear so. Women who
were charming but not helpless, like Angela Burdett Coutts,
Georgina and Mary Boyle, he was fond of but apparently never
obsessed by.)

What David says of his mother conceals from the reader – and
from David himself – what she really is. He is fascinated by her
and by her memory: 'Can I say of her innocent and girlish
beauty, that it faded, and was no more, when its breath falls on
my cheek now, as it fell that night? Can I say she ever changed,
when my remembrance brings her back to life, thus only? and,
truer to its loving youth than I have been, or man ever is, still
holds fast what it has cherished then?' But in her weakness and
timidity she neglects her duty to her child as surely as Mrs
Jellyby and Mrs Pocket, and what she calls affection for her
husband is rejection for her son. He comes back to a home
changed not only by his stepfather's open rejection of him, but
also by his mother's tacit acceptance of her husband's hostility.
He has lost his home, and his mother acquiesces in this too.

> God help me, I might have been improved for my whole life, I
> might have been made another creature perhaps for life, by a
> kind word at that season. A word of encouragement and
> explanation, of pity for my childish ignorance, of welcome
> home, might have made me dutiful to him in my heart hence-
> forth. . . . I thought my mother was sorry to see me standing
> in the room so scared and strange, and that, presently, when I
> stole to a chair, she followed me with her eyes more sorrow-
> fully still – missing, perhaps, some freedom in my childish
> tread – but the word was not spoken, and the time for it
> was gone.

No word is spoken by the stepfather, but no word is spoken by
the mother either: she will make no protest against his cruelty to
her 'precious treasure, the dearest little fellow that ever was'.

It is a fearful irony, not of course perceived by David, and
perhaps not by Dickens, that what she says of herself when

Peggotty shows herself unfavourable to the projected marriage
is perfectly true, although it is used at the time as emotional
blackmail: 'Am I a naughty mama to you, Davy? Am I a nasty,
cruel, selfish, bad mama? Say I am, my child; say yes, dear child,
and Peggotty will love you, and Peggotty's love is a great deal
better than mine, Davy. I don't love you at all, do I?' She does not
love him: she is fond of him as though he were a toy, and even
this immature affection, all that is left in the child's life, becomes
furtive and weak.

> She turned round at the parlour door, in the dusk, and taking
> me in her embrace as she had been used to do, whispered me
> to love my new father and be obedient to him. She did this
> hurriedly and secretly, as if it were wrong, but tenderly; and
> putting out her hand behind her, held mine in it, until we
> came near to where he was standing in the garden, where she
> let mine go, and drew hers through his arm.

She has not had the courage to tell David herself of the marriage,
and when he is troubled by Peggotty's revelation of it she thinks
not of the child whose whole world has been destroyed, but of
her own peace of mind, and weakly blames both Peggotty and
David.

> 'This is your doing, Peggotty, you cruel thing . . . How can
> you reconcile it to your conscience, I wonder, to prejudice my
> own boy against me, or against anybody who is dear to
> me? . . . It's enough to distract me . . . In my honeymoon, too,
> when my most inveterate enemy might relent, one would
> think, and not envy me a little peace of mind and happiness.
> Davy, you naughty boy! Peggotty, you savage creature! Oh,
> dear me!' cried my mother, turning from one of us to the
> other, in her pettish, wilful manner, 'what a troublesome
> world this is, when one has the most right to expect it to be as
> agreeable as possible!'

There speaks Mrs Nickleby, twenty years younger than we
know her. The one thing for which Mrs Copperfield is prepared
to make some sort of feeble stand is her own position in the
household, usurped by Miss Murdstone, but she never makes
any protest against David's continued ill-treatment, nor his

'being daily more and more shut out and alienated'. When he is beaten she only stops her ears and cries; when his going to boarding-school is discussed by Mr and Miss Murdstone 'my mother had, of course, agreed with them'; when he is being punished she makes no attempt to see him, and will not even look at him when he comes to prayers. It is Peggotty who comforts him and whose love he relies on; although he does not know it, he has ceased to expect any loving care from his mother. 'She did not replace my mother; no one could do that, but she came into a vacancy in my heart, which closed upon her . . . '.

If we regard all this as an unconscious self-analysis we shall see that Dickens has brought David to a crisis which in most children has to be resolved very much earlier. The child finds himself suddenly in the midst of an oedipal situation, but there can be no struggle for the possession of the mother: the rival is too strong and the mother too rejecting. Normally the child is able to make an adjustment to this situation because he finds that although the father has exclusive sexual possession of the mother he too loves the child, and because the mother's love for the father does not deprive the child of her particular love for him.

Dickens' presentation of the father-figure as completely unloving and of the mother as sweet and affectionate entirely hides the true nature of the situation here: it is the *mother* who prevents the child from coming to terms with his life. Perhaps she cannot help it, perhaps she is really too timid, too immature, too uncertain of herself to make any attempt to understand or help the child; but the effect is the same as if she were deliberately rejecting him, and his position becomes intolerable. How is he to make it tolerable? He can of course reject the previously loved mother, but this is itself intolerable: the love relationship must be preserved as a matter of life or death, and of the various ways of doing this Dickens seems to have chosen to abandon the mother as she now appears in reality for the mother as she once appeared and as she is remembered.

We have seen how this happened in his life: his mother was regarded with indifference or dislike, but he was continually searching for, and captivated by, any girl resembling the young, charming, small and rather helpless figure of his earliest remembrance. In this particular situation in literature he resolves the problem very skilfully, although – or perhaps because – he still cannot face its essence: that the mother can really abandon the child to such unhappiness. So David is allowed to keep for ever the image of the loved and loving mother, with the image of himself eternally unseparated from her, while the wicked father suffers total loss. If the mother were to go on living, her rejection of the child would become apparent. David is already beginning to include her among those who make him unhappy: 'what a blank space I seemed, which *everybody* overlooked, and yet was in *everybody's* way' (my italics). She must die.

All this is perfectly explicit, even to David, when he sees his mother for the last time: although she is still alive, she is already frozen into the stillness of a memory.

> I kissed her and my baby brother, and was very sorry then; but not sorry to go away, for the gulf between us was there, and the parting was there, every day. . . . I was in the carrier's cart when I heard her calling to me. I looked out, and she stood at the garden gate alone, holding her baby up in her arms for me to see. It was cold, still weather, and not a hair of her head or a fold of her dress was stirred, as she looked intently at me, holding up her child. So I lost her. So I saw her afterwards in my sleep at school – a silent presence near my bed – looking at me with the same intent face – holding up the baby in her arms.

Forster's warning against reading *David Copperfield* only as an autobiographical novel is right enough. 'The *Copperfield* disclosures formerly made', he says, 'will forever connect the book with the author's individual story; but too much has been assumed, from these revelations, of a full identity of Dickens with his hero, and a supposed intention that his own character as well as parts of his career should be expressed in the narrative.'[37] The account of the factory episode of course, some mingling of fact and fancy in Mr Creakle's school and the short reference to the beginning of David's career as a journalist and writer are probably the only truly autobiographical parts of the novel until we come to the love affair with Dora. A good deal of his story here was no doubt derived from actual memories of the time when he was in love with Maria Beadnell; but he did not marry Maria, and David does marry Dora. Yet this passage is also autobiographical because it embodies what was happening in Dickens' unconscious mind: the search for the lost mother-figure. It is unlikely that he realised that Maria attracted him because she was like his mother, nor does he show any signs that he knows David to be in love with Dora for the same reason; yet the resemblances between Dora and Mrs Copperfield are so strongly implicit that we are forced to the conclusion that David is in fact marrying his mother and that the whole Dora episode is an exploration of what happens when this unconscious wish is fulfilled.

What happens is, naturally enough, that the whole mother–child relationship is repeated, though this time with the difference that David is husband, not child. His instantaneous falling in love shows the obsessional nature of his passion:

> All was over in a moment. I had fulfilled my destiny. . . . I was swallowed up in an abyss of love in an instant. There was no pausing on the brink; no looking down, or looking back; I was gone, headlong, before I had sense to say a word to her. . . . I don't think I had any definite idea where Dora came from, or in what degree she was related to a higher order of beings; but I am quite sure I should have scouted the notion of her being simply human, like any other young lady, with indignation and contempt.

David's feeling for Dora illustrates very well Jung's explanation of why maternally-deprived men choose this particular type of love-object: 'The feature of over-estimation by which the loved one becomes the unique, the irreplaceable one, fits just as readily into the infantile set of ideas, for no one possesses more than one mother, and the relation to her rests on an experience which is assured beyond all doubt, and can never be repeated.' It is no surprise to David, or indeed to the reader, to find Miss Murdstone there, his mother's old tormentor now become Dora's. The evenings with Peggotty are repeated too 'with the old set of industrial implements', but now talking about Dora, not his mother.

Miss Trotwood is again the voice of truth. 'You were not equally matched', she told David's mother, and now she tries to prevent David from making the mistake his father made:

> 'You mean to say the little thing is very fascinating, I
> suppose?'
> 'My dear aunt,' I replied, 'no-one can form the least idea
> what she is!'
> 'Ah! And not silly?' said my aunt.
> 'Silly, Aunt!'
> I seriously believe it had never once entered my head for a
> single moment, to consider whether she was or not. I
> resented the idea, of course; but I was in a manner struck by it,
> as a new one altogether.

He resents the idea, but he never examines it, and the question
whether Dora is silly is never answered by David, only by her
own behaviour. Her silliness makes her selfish and irresponsible: she is totally unable to face reality. When David's aunt has
lost her money and he has to get up early to go to work,
Dora is disturbed.

> She said to me, in her pretty coaxing way – as if I were a doll, I
> used to think! – 'Now, don't get up at five o'clock, you
> naughty boy. It's so nonsensical.'
> 'My love,' said I, 'I have work to do.'
> 'But don't do it!' returned Dora. 'Why should you?'
> It was impossible to say to that sweet little surprised face,
> otherwise than lightly and playfully, that we must work, to
> live.
> 'Oh! How ridiculous!' cried Dora.
> 'How shall we live without, Dora?' said I.
> 'How? Any how!' said Dora.
> She seemed to think she had quite settled the question, and
> gave me such a triumphant little kiss, direct from her
> innocent heart, that I would hardly have put her out of
> conceit with her answer, for a fortune.

Her retreat from reality extends over every facet of their life
together.

> 'My sweet, I am only going to reason.'
> 'Oh, but reasoning is worse than scolding!' exclaimed Dora,

in despair. 'I didn't marry to be reasoned with. If you meant to reason with such a poor little thing as I am, you ought to have told me so, you cruel boy.' . . .

'Dora, my darling!'

'No, I am not your darling. Because you *must* be sorry that you married me, or else you wouldn't reason with me!'

The parallel between Dora and David's mother is shown strongly by their using almost identical language. 'Whatever I am, I am affectionate,' says Mrs Copperfield. 'I know I am affectionate. I wouldn't say it if I wasn't certain that I am.' When David says to Dora that being treated rationally need not make her unhappy, she begins to sob, and her only defence against David's proposal is to say, 'I am sure I am very affectionate . . . you oughtn't to be cruel to me, Doady!' Miss Trotwood calls Mrs Copperfield 'a Baby', and Dora calls herself a child-wife, and of course what they both resist so fearfully is growing up. Their 'affection', if it exists at all, is purely need-love, which lives only to receive, to have its own needs and desires answered.

This is a perfectly proper kind of love for a child to feel; indeed it is only by receiving love that a child learns to give it, and only by having its own demands answered can it gradually learn to respond to the demands of others. But for an adult to remain fixated at this stage amounts precisely to a refusal, or an inability, to grow up and a demand to be treated as a child. Mrs Copperfield could only be treated as a naughty child by Murdstone because she acquiesces in this treatment, and Dora actually welcomes being spoiled.

Dora seemed, by one consent, to be regarded like a pretty toy or plaything. . . . It was very odd to me; but they all seemed to treat Dora, in her degree, much as Dora treated Jip in his. . . . I said to her that I wished she could get them to behave towards her differently. . . . 'I'm sure they're very kind to me,' said Dora, 'and I am very happy.'

David's attempt to 'form her mind' is of course doomed to failure, and so is his marriage, although this is never admitted in the novel. David attributes 'the old unhappy loss or want of something' to a conscious, not an unconscious disillusion.

> When I walked alone in the fine weather, and thought of the summer days when all the air had been filled with my boyish enchantment, I did miss something of the realisation of my dreams, but I thought it was a softened glory of the Past, which nothing could have thrown upon the present time. I did feel, sometimes, for a little while, that I could have wished my wife had been my counsellor; had had more character and purpose, to sustain me and improve me by; had been endowed with power to fill up the void which somewhere seemed to be about me; but I felt as if this were an unearthly consummation of my happiness, that never had been meant to be, and never could have been.

But he knows that there is a void which should not have been there and, in one of Dickens' extraordinary apprehensions of psychological truth, he connects its existence with the past and recognises that its 'filling up' never could have been, since it was in the past that the void grew and only then could it have been filled. The marriage partners fall into their rightful places: Dora as the pampered child and David, who had so much needed a mother, forced into the role of the unwilling parent. 'I bore the weight of all our little cares, and all my projects; Dora held the pens; and we both felt that our shares were adjusted as the case required.'

Of course Dora must die: not, as the Leavises say, that 'the little Blossom withers away in the unsuccessful attempt to become a mother'[38] (since being a mother is unfortunately not at all incompatible with emotional immaturity, as in the case of David's mother). No: it is because if Mrs Copperfield lives she must become Mrs Nickleby, and if Dora lives she must become Flora Finching. It is only youth and prettiness which hide the essential failure to develop their characters; once these have gone the preoccupations with self and with trivial concerns which are so delightful in a child, because they are the means to growth, are revealed for what they are: the stultifying of every possibility.

It seems however that Dickens still only knew this unconsciously, since he did not meet Maria Winter (*née* Beadnell) until six years later, and it is only too obvious that he expected time to have made very little difference to her and felt that it had made no difference at all to his own feelings:

These are things that I have locked up in my own breast and that I never thought to bring out any more. But when I find myself writing to you again 'all to yourself', how can I forbear to let as much light upon them as will shew you that they are still there! If the most innocent, the most ardent, and the most disinterested days of my life had you for their sun – as indeed they had . . . how can I receive a confidence from you, and return it, and make a feint of blotting all this out![39]

But when he did meet her he was staggered to find that the 'spoiled and artless' charm of his former love depended entirely on youth and prettiness; without these, she meant nothing to him.

Dickens' unconscious association of his mother and Maria Beadnell is shown in the resemblance between Mrs Nickleby and Flora, two characters based on the two real women. One character is an early creation, the other a product of matured genius at its height, but the link between them is their conversational style. Flora however has a warmth, a good-heartedness, a real feeling of affection towards Arthur and Little Dorrit in spite of her concern for her own comfort which Dickens certainly did not find in Maria Winter, whom he did his best to avoid after his disillusionment. This may suggest, if not a reconciliation with the silly charmer whom age through no fault of her own has deprived of charm, at least a lessening of bitterness.

Finally, with the figure of Mrs Lirriper, the last of the stream-of-consciousness talkers, in the situation of which she is the centre, we have the nearest approach Dickens can make to a reconciliation with his own childhood and with the elements of which it was composed. Mrs Lirriper is 'silly', as Mrs Nickleby and Flora were: that is, her conversational style perpetually running on in a mass of free associations shows her mind to be concerned with an enormous number of trivialities, but at the same time the warmth and helpfulness which find no true outlet in Flora deepen into an undercurrent of steady faithfulness and love which save both Major Jackman and the boy Jemmy. Mrs Lirriper when young and goodlooking marries a John-Dickens-type husband, 'a handsome figure of a man, and a man with a jovial heart and a sweet temper . . . a beaming eye and a voice as mellow as a musical instrument made of honey and steel, but he

had ever been a free liver', and when he dies in the second year
of their marriage, 'being behindhand with the world', she works
for years to pay off his debts and then takes on another dependent of the same kind: the Major, with his gentlemanly
behaviour and his love of orotund speeches, 'punctual in all
respects except one irregular which I need not particularly
specify'.

The Mrs Copperfield figure is represented by young Mrs
Edson 'with her pretty bright hair blowing this way and that'.
She too is only a baby, 'much more like a little affectionate half-
broken-hearted child than ever I can imagine any grown
person', and being quite unable to cope with adult life, in which
she has been betrayed by her lover, she too dies. Her character
is barely sketched, since she exists only to bear a child for Mrs
Lirriper and the Major; and although they are only surrogate
parents they save the child from being a foundling like Oliver
Twist, a factory child like David, a child riddled with guilt for
having been born like Esther Summerson, a victim of harshness
and injustice like Pip – all the unwanted children that Dickens
ever wrote about are redeemed in Jemmy. Only it is not a real
coming to terms with the situation because Jemmy's salvation is
achieved at the cost of a lie. Mrs Lirriper and the Major have
never dared to tell Jemmy his story and are terrified that he shall
find it out, since his own watchword is 'Unchanging Love and
Truth'. When it becomes obvious that he has no knowledge of
the secret, Mrs Lirriper says, 'I felt that we were almost safe now,
I felt that the dear boy had no suspicion of the bitter truth, and I
looked at the Major for the first time and drew a long breath.'
The truth is so bitter that it is seen as dangerous, and the boy's
apparent security rests on insecurity.

The Leavises recognise very well that because 'David's love of
his mother is the love of Woman, . . . he is always looking for her
image, a pettish, wilful, childish, loving playmate',[40] and that
therefore this sets the pattern of his emotional life. But their
application of this theme to Dickens' life seems to me to go
astray because they place it on the level of conscious delibera-
tion rather than of unconscious and compulsive need. They
say:

> Idealizing immaturity stabilized it and inhibited maturity in
> women, but this was not the product of a morbid and

irrational desire in the man since the qualities that Dickens
shows as being associated with feminine immaturity of the
Clara–Em'ly–Dora kind represented a real emotional need
for men living in the world that the 19th century became.
... Of course the dilemma was that the qualities needed in a
satisfactory wife (as efficient household manager and
mother) were of a conflicting kind with the other need.[41]

This may be true, in the sense that in every age some men are
looking for child-wives, and perhaps there were more of these
in the Victorian age than in some other ages, but I doubt
whether it could be substantiated in any useful way. The literature of the period does not uphold such claims. If we leave out
the female novelists and poets, whom we may expect to be
biased, there is no plethora of child-wives in Bulwer-Lytton,
Kingsley, Trollope, Hughes, Wilkie Collins – certainly not in
Browning, Tennyson or Patmore. Thackeray did have an
Amelia, but that was because he suffered from an inner compulsion somewhat similar to that of Dickens. Ruskin and Lewis
Carroll, who were attracted by young girls, rather disliked the
triviality of childhood and did their best to make their girl com-
panions wise and mature, in everything except physique; they
wanted adult children, not child adults.

The Hollywood cinema of the thirties and forties and televi-
sion drama of our own day is fuller of baby-doll characters than
Victorian fiction. In this area, as in many others, Dickens has
stamped his own impress so deeply that the child-wife, the
vapid and immature girl, has become the type of the Victorian
heroine. And yet this is not such a large area, even in his own
work; he explores the adult child just as closely as he does the
child adult.

If the dilemma which Dickens was trying to resolve were on
such a conscious level as the Leavises posit, there would have
been no difficulty. He could have married his 'childish, loving
playmate' and hired a competent housekeeper. He did in fact
acquire in Georgina a very capable housekeeper, hostess and
nurse for his children, so that he did not have the practical difficulties with his household which made David's life with Dora
difficult. But this had no effect at all on his inner restlessness,
which came from his early maternal deprivation and to which
the only answer was in the past. Dora's own epitaph upon

herself shows that Dickens knew this, and his presentation of the failure of David's attempt to replace his mother by Dora shows his realisation that such an attempt is basically hopeless. In the novel he solves David's problem by giving him a real, 'good' mother-figure in Agnes. (Her parental status is shown by David's referring to her as 'the dear presence without which I were nothing', just as he formerly referred to his father as 'the dust that once was he, without whom I had never been'.)

The marriage to Agnes rounded the novel off well, it satisfied the Victorian reader's desire for a spiritual marriage which should yet be highly fertile, and it may have proved a sop to Georgina's desire for some recognition of her devotion to Dickens and his family, if she needed one. But that it did not satisfy Dickens' own inner need is shown by the fact that he returns to almost the same theme in *Little Dorrit*. The difference is that this time Arthur Clennam is not an inexperienced boy falling in love for the first time, but a disillusioned man of forty. Dickens was forty-three, and it is easy to see a good deal of self-portraiture in Clennam, a man who has had no opportunity to develop a true self because he has been forced to become what his parents made him, with 'a void' in his 'cowed heart' and 'a nature that had been disappointed from the dawn of its perceptions'. We have in him also the memory of his passionate boyish love for Flora (Flora being, of course, Dickens' portrait of the middle-aged Maria Winter, who had been Maria Beadnell).

Clennam is attracted to Pet Meagles, another Dora, 'a fair girl with rich brown hair hanging free in natural ringlets . . . ; she was round and fresh and dimpled and spoilt, and there was in Pet an air of timidity and dependence which was the best weakness in the world, and gave her the only crowning charm a girl so pretty and pleasant could have been without.' And we are specifically told that when Affery mentions Flora to Clennam, 'she had introduced into the web that his mind was busily weaving, in that old workshop where the loom of his youth had stood, the last thread wanting to the pattern', and he realises that 'the face of the pretty girl from whom he had parted with regret, had had an unusual interest for him, and a tender hold upon him, because of some resemblance, real or imagined, to this first face that had soared out of his gloomy life into the bright glories of fancy'. It is a great temptation here to say that *Dickens didn't know it*, but Clennam was really looking for the face of his young mother, the 'little beauty' from whom he had been separated before his earliest memories began.

Dickens put a great deal of his own feelings at this time into the character of Clennam. He described himself as 'never at rest, and never satisfied, and ever trying after something that is never reached'.[42] His recent disillusion over Maria Winter had made him feel that what he was searching for never could be found and, like Dora, he speaks of himself as past: 'one happiness I have missed in life, and one friend and companion I never made'.[43] This elegiac note is echoed in the chapters on Clennam's unfulfilled love for Pet (which are curiously proleptic, since they describe accurately what Dickens must have felt on realising that he was in love with Ellen Ternan, whom he was to meet a few months later).

If Clennam had not decided against falling in love with Pet; if he had had the weakness to do it; if he had, little by little, persuaded himself to set all the earnestness of his nature, all the might of his hope, and all the wealth of his matured character, on that cast; if he had done this and found that all was lost; he would have been, that night, unutterably miserable. As it was – As it was, the rain fell heavily, drearily.

Dickens again connects Clennam's 'very sharp' pain, although it is directly due to his hopeless love for Pet, with his past by describing it as 'peculiar as his life and history'. And on the evening of Pet's engagement to Gowan, 'he became in his own eyes, as to any similar hope or prospect, a very much older man who had done with that part of life'. The roses which had symbolised that love float away on the river of time, back into the past, 'and thus do greater things that once were in our breasts, and near our hearts, flow from us to the eternal seas'.

Although the David–Dora–Agnes situation is to some extent repeated here, Dickens knows now that marriage to the pretty spoiled child is no way to fill 'the empty place in his heart that he has never known the meaning of', but he can see no other cure for Clennam's unhappiness than again to marry him to the girl who has been a parent to her own father, as Agnes was. But he knew that this was not really his answer, and perhaps it is not an unreasonable assumption that to have got so far in his unconscious self-analysis and to have come to a dead end was the cause of the frenzy of misery and restlessness which fell upon him after *Little Dorrit* was finished. 'I must do *something,* or I shall wear my heart away';[44] 'Am altogether in a dishevelled state of mind – notes of new books in the dirty air, miseries of older growth threatening to close upon me';[45] 'I have rested nine or ten weeks, and sometimes feel as if it had been a year – though I had the strangest nervous miseries before I stopped. If I couldn't walk fast and far, I should just explode and perish';[46] 'I have now no relief but in action, I am become incapable of rest'.[47]

He did not touch the direct theme of the search for the mother again until its final and profound exploration in *Great Expectations.* But the theme of the empty heart in its hopeless search for love does occur in the Christmas Number of *Household Words* for 1857 (six months after *Little Dorrit* was finished) and in *A Tale of Two Cities* (1858). In the Christmas Number, *The Perils of Certain English Prisoners*, the two chapters which Dickens wrote contain a love story almost entirely unrelated to the central action, which concerns the capture by pirates of a party of marines and some of the members of a British colony on an island in the Caribbean, and their subsequent escape. One of the marines falls in love with a sister of one of his officers, whom he has of course no hope of marrying.

The episode seems to be introduced merely to express some of the despair and frustration which Dickens must have been feeling if he was, as seems likely, in love with Ellen Ternan at this time. Again we have the positive identification of the misery of unrequited love with the misery of early experiences. 'After I had left them, I laid myself down on my face on the beach, and cried for the first time since I had frightened birds as a boy. . . . I . . . fell asleep with wet eyelashes and a sore, sore heart. Just as I had often done when I was a child, and had been worse used than usual.' And there is no substitute love for him; for the first time Dickens shows the desolation of total loss. 'I well knew what an immense distance there was between me and Miss Maryon; . . . I well knew that she was as high above my head as the sky over my head; and yet I loved her. . . . I suffered agony – agony. I suffered hard and I suffered long.' He lives out his life in this sorrow and it is only when he is old, and 'all my old pain has softened away', that he becomes a servant in the household of his former love, herself happily married.

Time is the only cure that Dickens can now see for pain of this kind, but there is one more remedy: death. This is the only way in which Sydney Carton will ever be free from the ache of his unreturned passion. Carton resembles Clennam in that his life has been blighted, 'waste forces within him, and a desert all around'. Did Dickens haunt Ellen Ternan's house as Carton haunted Lucie's?

> Many a night he vaguely and unhappily wandered there . . . ; many a dreary daybreak revealed his solitary figure lingering there, and still lingering there when the first beams of the sun brought into strong relief, removed beauties of architecture in spires of churches and lofty buildings, as perhaps the quiet time brought some sense of better things, else forgotten and unattainable, into his mind.

Did he say to her (knowing that he could never be free to marry her) what Carton says to Lucie: 'If it had been possible . . . that you could have returned the love of the man you see before you . . . he would have been conscious this day and hour, in spite of his happiness, that he would bring you to misery, bring you to sorrow and repentance, blight you, disgrace you, pull you down with him'? Clennam, Carton, Dickens – all felt their lives to be a ruined waste untouched by anything living; all of them could say, at the birth of hopeless love, 'I have had the weakness . . . to wish you to know with what a sudden mastery you kindled me, heap of ashes that I am, into fire – a fire, however, inseparable in its nature from myself, quickening nothing, lighting nothing, doing no service, idly burning away.' (Dickens uses the same metaphor, with greater force, in *Hard Times* when Louisa says, 'There seems to be nothing there but languid and monotonous smoke. Yet when the night comes, Fire bursts out . . . !')

Carton makes the same identification between sorrow and the past when, thinking of Lucie and his approaching renunciation of life for her sake, he says to Mr Lorry, 'Does your childhood seem far off? Do the days when you sat at your mother's knee, seem days of very long ago?' Mr Lorry has happy remembrances of childhood and says to Carton, 'but you . . . you are young'. 'Yes,' answers Carton bitterly, 'I am not old, but my young way was never the way to age.' The theme of the death of the true self is symbolised in *David Copperfield* by the death of David's baby brother: 'The mother who lay in the grave, was the mother of my infancy, the little creature in her arms was myself, as I had been once, hushed for ever on her bosom.' In *Little Dorrit* Clennam has, unknown to himself, been torn from his young and loving mother, so that his nature 'had been disappointed from the dawn of its perceptions' and his childhood became nothing but 'the void in my cowed heart'. Carton delivers the final words on this theme, spoken with a conscious meaning, but full of deep unconscious truth: 'I am like one who died young. All my life might have been.'

3

Against Peace, against Hope, against Happiness

It seems to be too painful for Dickens to accept the idea of the rejecting mother directly, so that he has to approach it obliquely: either he follows the tradition of folklore by using the stepmother concept (that is, the one who rejects the child is a mother-substitute, not the true parent) or he refuses to take the rejection seriously by treating it as comedy. The true mother is always seen by Dickens as loving the child even though, as in *David Copperfield*, she really fails him or, as in *Nicholas Nickleby*, she is totally self-concerned and incapable of love. (In this early book he cannot manage his two worlds as skilfully as in later works: although Mrs Nickleby is a purely comic figure, he feels constrained to add the occasional disruptive sentimentality such as the awkward scene in which Mrs Nickleby's masterly reflections on the silver tea-pot with the ivory knob and the spice-box which 'used to stand in the left-hand corner, next but two to the pickled onions' are suddenly broken in upon by Kate's maunderings about her father's death – 'the kindest and gentlest heart that ever ached on earth has passed in peace to heaven' – and immediately followed by a moral discourse beginning: 'It is an exquisite and beautiful thing in our nature, that when the heart is touched and softened by some tranquil happiness or affectionate feeling, the memory of the dead . . .' and so on.)

Sally Brass, the most violently rejecting of mothers, who hates and ill-treats her child, is no mother at all in the final version – or at least her maternity is barely hinted at: 'Sophronia herself supposed she was an orphan; but Mr Swiveller, putting various slight circumstances together, often thought Miss Brass must know better than that.' Mrs Tetterby (with every excuse of poverty and overcrowding) rejects her children only under Redlaw's enchantment. Old Mrs Brown, however criminal her

47

life and activities, really loves her daughter. Even the wilderness
Mrs Skewton makes of her daughter's life is due to a mistaken
desire for her own and Edith's security; when she is dying she
longs for her daughter's love: ' "Why are you so unmoved? . . .
It turns me cold to see you sitting at my side." "I am sorry,
mother." "Sorry! You seem always sorry. But it is not for me!"
With that she cries . . . ' . And the moment of death brings a kind
of reconciliation, as she remembers a time when she and Edith
did love each other: 'Her wandering hands upon the coverlet
join feebly palm to palm, and move towards her daughter; and a
voice not like hers, not like any voice that speaks one mortal
language – says, "For I nursed you." '

It is easy to see how Dickens' treatment of the two mothers
who really reject their children, Mrs Jellyby and Mrs Pocket,
could have been entirely different. Given a serious viewpoint –
and they are (by Dickens' standards of naturalism) naturalis-
tically treated – the plight of the children in these homes could
be as heartbreaking as that of David Copperfield; but it never is
treated seriously. The mothers' attitudes to their children are
observed humorously and without involvement, so that we cannot help but regard them as comic. There is, to be sure, a touch of
true pathos in Peepy, 'so cold that his teeth were chattering as if
he had cut them all' or dipping Noah into the wine glasses at the
wedding breakfast, but it is never developed.

Mrs Jellyby is indifferent to her children, Mrs Pocket is hostile
to hers. When given the baby, she 'got its head upon the table;
which was announced to all present by a prodigious concus-
sion', and later she allows it to do 'most appalling things with the
nutcrackers'. When the little girl Jane coaxes this dangerous
implement away from the baby,

> Mrs Pocket . . . not approving of this, said to Jane: 'You
> naughty child, how dare you? Go and sit down this
> instant!' . . .
> Mrs Pocket's dignity was so crushing, that I felt quite abashed:
> as if I myself had done something to rouse it.
> 'Belinda,' remonstrated Mr Pocket from the other end of the
> table, 'how can you be so unreasonable? Jane only interfered
> for the protection of the baby.'
> 'I will not allow anybody to interfere,' said Mrs Pocket. 'I am

surprised, Mathew, that you should expose me to the affront of interference.'

'Good God!' cried Mr Pocket, in an outbreak of desolate desperation. 'Are infants to be nutcrackered into their tombs, and is nobody to save them?'

The answer is that infants are not to be nutcrackered into their tombs *in this chapter*, because Mrs Pocket is a comic character and so (presumably) is the baby. But *Great Expectations* is nonetheless a book about the absolute helplessness of the child in an adult world. Pip is helpless in the face of his sister's cruelty, Estella is helpless when, at the age of three, she is torn from her murderess mother and convict father and handed over to a severely disturbed mother-substitute. But Dickens does, for the first and, I think, the only time, take this situation one step further. It is not so much the sins of the fathers that are visited on the children, but the wrongs of those fathers.

Dickens tells us nothing about Mr Dombey's or Miss Barbary's childhood (though Mrs Clennam says of herself, 'The corruption of our hearts, the evil of our ways, the curse that is upon us, the terrors that surround us – these were the themes of my childhood'). But Pip is delivered over to his sister's brutality because Joe has been conditioned by *his* father's brutality: 'I see so much in my poor mother, of a woman drudging and slaving and breaking her honest hart and never getting no peace in her mortal days, that I'm dead afeered of going wrong in the way of not doing what's right by a woman, and I'd far rather of the two go wrong the t'other way, and be a little ill-convenienced myself.' Estella is what she is partly because her father was 'a ragged little creature as much to be pitied as ever I see'. Even Mrs Pocket cannot, in a sense, help being unloving and useless, because that is what she was brought up to be.

Because Dickens is exploring here what he does remember, a child's helplessness in the face of misery brought on him by adult cruelty or neglect, *Great Expectations* comes nearer than any other book to exploring what he does not remember, his mother's early rejection of him and his passionate need to repeat the pattern of that rejection. But as we have seen, his feelings about motherhood are ambivalent (because of his conscious dislike of his mother and his unconscious desire for the early relationship between them). So while it is a critical truism that there are very few 'good' mothers in Dickens, it is also true that there are no 'bad' ones; it seems as if, while he does not know how to write about good mothering, he finds it too painful to describe the real rejection of a child by its mother. Sally Brass, as I have said, is not the Marchioness's mother in the final version, and the first book explicitly about parental rejection concerns a father and child (Florence's mother and stepmother both love her more than they love her father). Even Dr Marigold's wife, who beats her child cruelly in uncontrollable fits of temper, really loves and takes great care of it.

The good mothers and the bad are surrogates. In *David Copperfield* it is only the Murdstones, incapable of any kind of humanity, who are hostile to David, and Dickens avoids the sensitive area by not admitting his mother's betrayal of him (though it is plain to the reader). Caddy Jellyby and Arthur Clennam are wounded by the indifference or hostility of their respective mothers, but they are at least adults, and their pain is not the helpless intolerable suffering of children – and Arthur's mother, besides, turns out not to be his real mother. So it is not surprising that when Dickens does bring himself to explore from the inside rejection of the child by one who *ought* to love him, he cannot, now or ever, face the possibility of rejection by the mother.

Pip's sister is the only mother he has ever known, but she rejects, not only him, but the whole relationship; she has brought him up from a sense of duty, not because she loves him – indeed, she appears to feel for him nothing but dislike and hostility.

> 'I have only been to the churchyard,' said I, from my stool, crying and rubbing myself.
> 'Churchyard!' repeated my sister. 'If it warn't for me you'd have been to the churchyard long ago, and stayed there. Who brought you up by hand?'
> 'You did,' said I.
> 'And why did I do it, I should like to know?' exclaimed my sister.
> I whimpered, 'I don't know.'
> '*I* don't,' said my sister. 'I'd never do it again. I know that. I may truly say I've never had this apron of mine off, since born

you were. It's bad enough to be a blacksmith's wife (and him a
Gargery), without being your mother.'

She is, in fact, in the position of a woman forced to have a child
she does not want, and it is with extraordinary ingenuity that
Dickens has managed to create this situation, which must have
been crucial to him, without putting the woman and child in the
much more painful relationship of mother and son. Yet since
Mrs Joe is so unloving and aggressive, it is not unlikely that her
mother was the same and that she is in effect merely repeating
the experience that Pip would have undergone in any case.

In *David Copperfield* it is very clear to the reader that David is
attracted to Dora because she resembles his mother – not only
in manner and temperament, but in her practice of emotional
blackmail – but we have no means of knowing whether it was
clear to Dickens. The Leavises think that he 'was in firm control
of his theme'[1] and that the presence of Miss Murdstone at
David's first meeting with Dora 'made the parallel of Clara
Copperfield and Dora Spenlow inescapable for the original
readers'.[2] I am not so sure of this: I think it much more likely
that, as often happened, Dickens' theme was in firm control of
him and that he was unaware of what he was doing. Certainly
his 'original readers' seem to have been entirely unaware of it:
there are no early references at all, that I have been able to find,
to the identification of Clara and Dora.

But in *Great Expectations*, although I think he is still largely
unconscious of the implications of Pip's need to repeat the
pattern of his first emotional experience in his attachment to
Estella, there are signs that his unconscious mind is pushing him
very much more strongly to make an unmistakable identification
between Estella and Mrs Joe. Again and again in crucial scenes
there are cross-references, for which there is no reason in the
plot and which have the sole function of linking the two women.
And yet, though these links seem perfectly explicit, I must
repeat that I think they were made by the unconscious
knowledge struggling to emerge into consciousness; I do not
believe that Dickens knew either that there was any connection
between Estella and Mrs Joe, or that his theme was again the
fatal tendency for the child deprived of maternal affection to
repeat the pattern of his first relationship with the mother-
figure.

Pip's sister is scornful, unjust and destructive of his confidence and of his sense of himself as a person rather than an object; so when he meets these qualities allied to youth, beauty and an elevated social status, he is utterly lost, as David was with Dora. Herbert says to him: 'When you told me your own story, you told me plainly that you began adoring her the first time you saw her, when you were very young indeed.' And after that first meeting – at which, we observe, she has not charmed him nor made herself attractive to him, but has merely reinforced what he is always being made to feel ('I was so humiliated, hurt, spurned, offended, angry, sorry – I cannot hit upon the right name for the smart – God knows what its name was – that tears started to my eyes') – it is his life with his sister that springs to his mind in his bitter struggle with his feelings.

> My sister's bringing-up had made me sensitive. In the little world in which children have their existence, whosoever brings them up, there is nothing so finely perceived and finely felt, as injustice. . . . Within myself, I had sustained from my babyhood, a perpetual conflict with injustice. I had known, from the time when I could speak, that my sister, in her capricious and violent coercion, was unjust to me.

Yes; but how has Estella been unjust to him in that one meeting, so that he is inevitably reminded of his sister? Mrs Joe is certainly unjust in that she often assumes innocent actions to be guilty ones, but Estella has not done that. Is it not plain that the injustice they have both committed is the greatest of all, that of *not loving* him? Unrequited love appears even to adults not only as a grief but also as a wrong. To a child it is a wrong, because the child needs love as he needs food and air, so that he may develop emotionally as well as physically. (Miss Havisham is a symbol of the crippling effect on the emotional life of rejection: she needed, as the child needs, not only to be loved but to have her love accepted.)

But there is another likeness between Estella and Mrs Joe which Dickens does not, I think, realise even unconsciously – although he might well have done so, since he found himself so often in the same situation with his own children. This is that Pip has been forced upon them both. They do not want him, he is a nuisance and a burden to them (as Dickens often felt his children were to him: 'Why was I ever a father? Why was *my* father ever a father?'³ 'I have some idea . . . of interceding with the Bishop of London to have a little service in Saint Paul's beseeching that I may be considered to have done enough towards my country's population.'⁴).

Pip cannot conceal from himself that Estella only keeps up her acquaintance with him because (as he thinks) Miss Havisham has ordered her to do so: 'Her manner was more winning than she had cared to let it be to me before, and I thought I saw Miss Havisham's influence in the change', and 'she drew her arm through mine, as if it must be done'. Even when her manner changes, he can never persuade himself that this is because she feels any affection for him:

> It was impossible for me to avoid seeing that she cared to attract me; that she made herself winning; and would have won me even if the task had needed pains. Yet this made me none the happier, for, even if she had not taken that tone of our being disposed of by others, I should have felt that she held my heart in her hand because she wilfully chose to do it, and not because it would have wrung any tenderness in her, to crush it and throw it away.

Neither Estella nor Mrs Joe has the slightest consideration for Pip as a person in his own right. The pattern connecting them is underlined by the disdain with which both of them give food to Pip and, more significantly, in the two fights, between Pip and Herbert and between Joe and Orlick. This is emphasised by Pip himself: 'Orlick, *as if he had been of no more account than the pale young gentleman* [my italics] was very soon among the coaldust, and in no hurry to come out.' Joe and Orlick get on well enough both before and after the fight: it is Mrs Joe who manoeuvres them into fighting, and who appears to derive from it the sexual satisfaction which her husband is incapable of giving her. Did Estella too leave the garden gate open hoping that the two boys would meet and find themselves rivals? Pip is ambiguous on this question: 'It is not much to the purpose whether a gate in that garden wall which I had scrambled up to peep over on the last occasion was, on that last occasion, open or shut. Enough that I saw no gate then, and that I saw one now. As it stood open, and as I knew that Estella had let the visitors out – for she had returned with the keys in her hand – I strolled into the garden.' She too shows signs of sexual excitement after the fight: 'there was a bright flush upon her face, as though something had happened to delight her. Instead of going straight to the gate, too, she stepped back into the passage and beckoned me: "Come here! You may kiss me if you like." '

'It is inevitable', says Edgar Johnson, 'that we should associate Pip's helpless enslavement to Estella with Dickens' desperate passion for Ellen Lawless Ternan.'[5] It would be more accurate, I think, to say that Dickens' passion for Ellen and Pip's passion for Estella both stem from the same root: Dickens' unconscious search for maternal love, 'seized and rended' by his unconscious need to perpetuate the pattern of maternal rejection. He was imprisoned on a fearful treadmill: he desperately needed to love only the kind of woman who could not give him what he desperately needed. We know little about his liaison with Ellen Ternan. There is some evidence that she was unhappy in it and, if my thesis is right, it could not give Dickens what he wanted, since what he wanted was in the past – and in the last novels, as I shall show, the compulsive obsessions reappear. Whatever solace the affair brought him, it could not assuage his terrible craving.

'The book will be written in the first person throughout,'[6] Dickens wrote to Forster, and of course there was no other way for him to explore himself. But the method has one defect that also, paradoxically enough, adds to its profound truth. This is that we never see Mrs Joe or Estella through any eyes but those of Pip. We never have a third-person narrator to tell us what they are really like in themselves. That there is another side to Mrs Joe we can guess: we see the tragedy of her life, her frustration in her marriage, perhaps the disappointment of her own childlessness, her really heroic struggle to bring up 'by hand' an unwanted baby brother while still a young girl herself, her narrow life of poverty and hard work. But Pip cannot see any of this, because no child can see his mother as a person in her own right nor in any other relation but her relation to him.

And Estella is even more enigmatic, to him and to us. Her story, for him, is merely the story of his own obsession with her. Even when, very occasionally, she reveals her own feelings, she is as much a mystery to us as to him. When she talks of her defenceless childhood passed among the machinations of Miss

Havisham's self-seeking relations, is her desire that they shall be thwarted the reason for her laughing 'with real enjoyment' at the idea of their hatred for Pip; or is she herself amused at Pip's error in supposing himself to be Miss Havisham's heir? If she dislikes Camilla for being hypocritical and time-serving, why does she despise Mathew Pocket for being neither? Does she ever, in any sense, care for Pip or even like him? She says that she deceives and entraps everyone but him, but Pip himself says, 'She cared to attract me', 'she lured me on', and she tortures him by making use of her familiarity with him to torment her other lovers. Her reason for marrying Bentley Drummle seems inadequate: 'I am tired of the life I have led, which has very few charms for me, and I am willing enough to change it.'

Then what kind of life would have charms for her? What are her aims, her motives, her pleasures, her interests? Is she as brainless and frivolous as Dora? She has the insight to see that Miss Havisham's feverish love for her is all self-indulgence, that she cannot feel love because she has never given any, and perhaps she feels some resentment; apart from this we know nothing of her as a person, and nor does Pip. For him she is Circe, the Siren, the Lorelei, Rappacini's Daughter, all myths of alluring and unattainable love, so that it is a shock to the reader when Herbert, who is not one of her victims, coolly reduces her to the level of an ordinary girl: 'She's a Tartar. . . . That girl's hard and haughty and capricious to the last degree.' She would be as effectively lost to Pip if she married him as she is when she marries Drummle, since her rejection of his love is as disastrously necessary to him as that love itself.

It is to this point in his unconscious self-analysis that *Great Expectations* has brought Dickens. And it is from this point that he explores Pip's hopeless love for Estella – hopeless not as Tom Pinch's love for Mary or Clennam's love for Pet were hopeless: with them it was merely the chance that Mary loved Martin and Pet loved Gowan that deprived them of happiness. But Pip's love is absolute despair, because whether or not it is successful, he knows that there is nothing in Estella to love or be loved. He has no illusions. 'The unqualified truth is, that when I loved Estella with the love of a man, I loved her simply because I found her irresistible. Once for all; I knew to my sorrow, often and often, if not always, that I loved her against reason, against promise, against

peace, against hope, against happiness, against all discourage-
ment that could be.'

This theme is repeated again and again with the inevitability
of Dickens' despairing letters to Forster about his own misery:
'Everything in our intercourse did give me pain. Whatever her
tone with me happened to be, I could put no trust in it, and build
no hope on it; and yet I went on against trust and against hope.'
'And still I stood looking at the house, thinking how happy I
should be if I lived there with her, and knowing that I never was
happy with her, but always miserable.' 'I never had one hour's
happiness in her society, and yet my mind all round the four-
and-twenty hours was harping on the happiness of having her
with me unto death.'

Now it may be, as I said before, that Dickens' passion for Ellen
Ternan and Pip's passion for Estella derive from the same root;
but still, when Dickens writes of Pip's feelings he is writing of
something much deeper in himself than a late love-affair, and to
take a description of one for a description of the other, as
Johnson and other critics have done, is to make a complex
matter far too simple. There was no reason why he should
consciously feel Pip's despair and frustration about Ellen: he
was separated from his wife, he had enough money to provide a
separate establishment for Ellen, and though it might take time
to persuade her to become his mistress, it seems likely that he
did so. Whatever the conscious agonies and ecstasies of this
time may have been for Dickens, the rending misery of Pip's
passion and his own unconscious feelings were of a different
kind. Nor does it seem likely that Ellen resembled Estella in any
way, though again it is fashionable to accept that the fictitious
character is taken from the living girl.

But the whole essence of Estella's nature is that she is aloof,
remote, a *princesse lointaine*, a star for a moth to flutter about,
whereas Dickens was a patron of the Ternan family, and Kate
Perugini said that Ellen flattered Dickens: 'he was ever apprecia-
tive of praise . . . Who could blame her? He had the world at his
feet. She was a young girl of eighteen, elated and proud to be
noticed by him.'[7] No; it is not *this* relationship that Dickens is
describing when he writes, 'I fancied, as I looked at her, that I
slipped hopelessly back into the coarse and common boy again.
O the sense of distance and disparity that came upon me, and
the inaccessibility that came about her!' and 'If I had been her

secretary, steward, half-brother, poor relation . . . I could not have seemed to myself, further from my hopes when I was nearest to her.' Every association of Pip's with Estella is rooted in his childhood and he feels himself always a boy with her, while she is a woman, superior and remote – as a child might feel towards a mother whose love can never be his. When Pip says 'You are part of my existence, part of myself. You have been in every line I have ever read, since I first came here, the rough common boy whose poor heart you wounded even then. You have been in every prospect I have ever seen since . . . The stones of which the strongest London buildings are made, are not more real, or more impossible to be displaced by your hands, than your presence and influence have been to me, there and everywhere, and will be. Estella, to the last hour of my life, you cannot choose but remain part of my character, part of the little good in me, part of the evil', the words well up 'like blood from an inward wound'. They rise indeed from that wound inflicted on the child's inner self before his earliest memories began.

But this wound could bleed only into the unconscious mind, though it welled up symbolically in Dickens' work. There was no way to go more deeply into this theme. If what is loved is not lovable and cannot love in return, if water will not cure a man's thirst, if Adam forever longs for a Paradise forever lost, what is he to do? 'Pip's despairing and disillusioned obsession with Estella', as Edgar Johnson says, is 'the darkest emotional imprisonment of all',[8] and there is no way out of that prison. Dickens' falling in love with Ellen Ternan no doubt brought this psychological state to a crisis, but I do not agree with Johnson that 'his insistence that since that last night of *The Frozen Deep* he had "never known a moment's peace or content" centres his distress unmistakably not on the "domestic unhappiness" alone but on a person: "never was a man so seized and rended by one Spirit".'[9] On the contrary, Dickens' use of the word 'Spirit' seems to give the experience a subjective, not an objective source. Whatever he saw of Estella in Ellen came from himself, not from her.

This is why I cannot at all agree with those critics who say that after Estella Dickens' heroines take on a different stamp. There is no 'after Estella': she is a dead end, a peak, a grave. One can stay there or turn back, but there is no possible way to go on. Dickens might have gone on writing other books about other Estellas, but he did not. He turned back. Angus Wilson says, 'Since Bella Wilfer in his next novel, *Our Mutual Friend*, was to be an even more living development of the same qualities, we may attribute to Ellen Ternan the only directly autobiographical aspect of *Great Expectations* . . . '[10] but this is simply not true.

Bella Wilfer and Rosa Bud have nothing of Estella in them: they are 'pettish and wilful'; real girls with aims and motives and occupations, however trivial; lovable – if you happen to like pettish wilfulness – and able to love. They are a reversion to Dolly Varden–Clara–Dora with some limited potential for growth in Bella's case (or, if one can hardly call it growth, at least she learns to keep 'the doll's house' as Dora could not) and probably in Rosa's too. But after all, Pet Meagles was able to adjust to the difficulties of becoming Mrs Gowan: the potential for change is not a new development. There is nothing of the myth about them.

The novel form calls for a heroine, and this is the only kind of heroine Dickens knows. Estella has been the exception. She is a part of Pip's past because that is where the only object of his, and his creator's, lifelong search was to be found. Pip shows perfect psychological accuracy when, after he has lost Estella, he turns back to his own past, to Biddy, the only mother-substitute he has known, and speaks to her in the tone of a child asking its mother for comfort: 'if you can receive me like a forgiven child (and indeed I am as sorry, Biddy, and have as much need of a hushing voice and a soothing hand) . . . '. But Dickens is even more accurate than Pip: he knows intuitively that Pip has been so conditioned to rejection by his early experiences that the loving mother is not now what he needs: 'she was not mine – she was never to be mine. She might have been, but that was past!'

After Estella the theme of the search for the mother never occurs again as the main theme, though it reappears, and with fearful intensity, in Bradley Headstone and John Jasper and, to a lesser degree, in John Harmon and Eugene Wrayburn. It exists still in their creator but, after Estella, what more can he say about it? He can only repeat what he has already said, but even more desperately. Pip does salvage some sort of life after he has lost Estella (I am leaving out of consideration the superimposed 'happy' ending), but it is a vicarious one: his home is Herbert's, his child is Biddy's. But Headstone and Jasper have no hope:

their doomed love leads them only, and irrevocably, to death.

And Dickens himself? His health began from this time to deteriorate, and only the formidable will that had created and directed his second self enabled him to get through his arduous days; but if we speak of his inner self, there is a sense in which it is true to say that, after Estella, Dickens began to die.

4
My Wound of Love

It has often been said of Dickens that he cannot write about 'real' women. Angus Wilson speaks of 'the absence of any real sympathy with, or understanding for women' as the 'second great defect of the Dickensian universe'[1] (the first being obsession with childhood). Sympathy and understanding are adult attributes, and when Dickens writes about women he sees them as a child sees: with the limitations of that vision, but also with its fidelity to psychological truth. He sees them as types, not persons, and as types that attract or repel according to whether or not they respond to his own needs. His women tell us nothing about the feminine mind and heart, as Maggie Tulliver and Lucy Snowe do, but they tell us a great deal about Dickens' attitude to women.

All the women in his books, with a few exceptions, are aspects of the mother as the child sees her. A child whose emotional development has been normal is able as he matures to see women as human beings with personalities, needs and capabilities of their own; a child whose development is stunted continues to see women as mysterious and perhaps dangerous, 'good' or 'bad' as they respond to the demands of his own fantasy. In the early books most of the heroines are stock figures of Victorian melodrama, entirely devoid of personality and existing merely as a focus for the hero's affections; but they all have a strong element of the maternal in their composition. Little Nell is a mother to her grandfather, Madeline Bray to her father, Kate Nickleby looks after her own mother, Rose Maylie is to be a mother to Oliver, Ruth Pinch looks after Tom.

It is in *Barnaby Rudge* that we see the first foreshadowing of future types. Dolly Varden is obviously based on recollections of Maria Beadnell and is the prototype of Dora, Pet (perhaps), Bella and Rosa Bud. But the other heroine is Emma Haredale, and the relationship between these two is the first appearance of a rather strange and not entirely explicable theme which recurs with increasing intensity and with a continual change of viewpoint. Emma and Dolly are presented as contrasts: Emma tall, pale, stately and serious, Dolly short, plump, rosy and coquettish. Dolly, 'even in the sincerity and earnestness of her grief' (at being captured) displays 'a little winning pettishness'; but Emma, though her feelings are 'usually of a quieter kind than Dolly's', is described by Dennis as 'one of them fine, black-eyed, proud gals, as I wouldn't trust at such times with a knife too near 'em'. We have here perhaps the germ of Edith Dombey, who says to Carker in the hour of his anticipated triumph: 'Stand still! ... or I shall murder you!' But it is only a hint (although the rioters 'held her in some degree of dread' and 'believed she had a weapon hidden in her dress, and was prepared to use it'), and Emma reverts to a more simple maternal role, soothing and tending Dolly, who 'nestles' in her bosom 'all the livelong day'. She becomes the forerunner of all the maternal girls who comfort and sustain other, less self-reliant girls.

The Battle of Life, while it has no other interest, carries on this theme with a strange emphasis on the relationship of the two sisters Grace and Marion.* Grace at first appears the little mother type so ready, in Dickens, to sacrifice herself completely: 'Grace ... seemed, in her gentle care of her younger sister, and in the steadiness of her devotion to her, older than she was; ... Great character of mother, that, even in this shadow and faint reflection of it, purifies the heart, and raises the exalted nature nearer to the angels!' We appear to have an Agnes–Dora–David situation, in which the young man entrusts his child-fiancée to the sister who is always 'calm, serene and cheerful', with 'the face of some bright angel', and who, like Agnes, is herself in love with the young man; this same situation later occurs between Little Dorrit and Pet. But it is here given a surprising twist by the younger sister's being mature enough (or, a modern reader might think, manipulative enough) to sacrifice her own love to that of her sister.

Otherwise the relationship between the sisters foreshadows that between Ada and Esther in *Bleak House*. Grace admires Marion's youth and beauty as Esther does Ada's, and there appears to be the same almost passionate love between them.

---

* Michael Slater in *Dickens and Women* discusses Dickens' interest in 'sisterly affection', but does not explain the curiously passionate element always occurring on one side of the relationship.

When Grace, after a three years' absence on the part of Marion's lover, says, 'I shall tell Alfred, when I give you back to him, that you have loved him dearly all the time . . . ', Marion replies, 'Tell him . . . that I have loved *you* all the time, dearer and dearer every day: and O! how dearly now!' Even when Grace has a little daughter of her own, Marion has 'no rival – no successor' in her affection. Their meeting after a long separation holds all the tremulous agitation of Esther's reunion with Ada: 'O God! was it a vision that came bursting from the old man's arms, and with a cry, and with a waving of its hands, and with a wild precipitation of itself upon her in its boundless love, sank down in her embrace!' Compare this with the much later 'Oh, how happy I was, down upon the floor, with my sweet beautiful girl down upon the floor too . . . rocking me to and fro like a child, calling me by every tender name that she could think of, and pressing me to her faithful heart.'

Agnes marries David because Dora is dead, and Dora in dying has left him to her as 'a last charge'. Grace marries Alfred because Marion has disappeared and has left him as a 'sacred trust' to her. Maclise's final illustration shows not the married pair, but the sisters embraced like a pair of lovers; and this curious theme is taken up again in the relationship between Ada and Esther in *Bleak House*. Their love has in it not the faintest hint of sexuality,* but it has passion: Esther's feelings for Ada are far more passionate than her feelings for Woodcourt.

This is clearly shown in her meetings with Ada and with Allan after her disfigurement. She is so ravaged by conflicting emotions before meeting Ada that, after hurrying out to meet her upon the road, she rushes back and remains trembling behind her bedroom door until a quasi love scene takes place between them. When she sees Woodcourt she does turn away from him at first and puts her veil half down, but soon feels 'comfortable' enough to put it aside and talk easily to him. When he goes abroad she is already in love with him, but is able to joke with Ada and Caddy about whether his parting gift of flowers shows that he is in love with her or not. But when Ada marries

---

* In which, indeed, Dickens' characters are remarkably deficient. Carker is the only strongly sexual personality. Pecksniff and Quilp show sexual traits, and it is obviously Steerforth's sexuality which attracts and terrifies Emily, but we see nothing of it at first hand. The devouring need of Pip, Bradley and Jasper is not sexual in origin: that could be satisfied, the other cannot.

Richard and goes to live in Chancery Lane (where Esther will see her every day) Esther's grief is uncontrollable:

> I lingered for one more look of the precious face, which it seemed to rive my heart to turn from ... And when I got downstairs, oh, how I cried! It almost seemed to me that I had lost my Ada for ever. I was so lonely, and it was so blank without her, and it was so desolate to be going home with no hope of seeing her there, that I could get no comfort for a little while, as I walked up and down in a dim corner, sobbing and crying.

Or think of that other lament of hers: 'The days when I frequented that miserable corner which my dear girl brightened, can never fade in my remembrance. I never see it, and I never wish to see it now; I have been there only once since; but in my memory there is a mournful glory shining on the place, which will shine for ever.'

This is the language of passionate love; there is nothing like it between Maggie Tulliver and Lucy Deane, nor between Lucy Snowe and Paulina, strong though the affection between them may be. Is this Esther's lament for her lost daughter, as her mother laments for her? 'My child, my child ... For the last time! These kisses for the last time! These arms upon my neck for the last time!' Is Esther to be always the mother she has never had? Or is it Dickens' lament for his lost Mary, or for an unknown love? It is unmistakably, like that other moment when Clennam watches Pet's roses float away down the river and feels part of his life going with them, the language of the living heart and its loss.

Little Dorrit's feelings for Pet and Lizzie Hexam's for Bella may hold the germ of that stronger relationship, but it never develops. In *Edwin Drood*, however, there is a similar situation which is evidently going to play an important part: Helena's instant attraction to Rosa. There is certainly an element of the maternal in it, but it is the fiercely protective, passionate emotion of a tigress defending its young. Rosa recognises and, in a sense, exploits this: 'I am such a mite of a thing, and you are so womanly and handsome. You seem to have resolution and power enough to crush me. I shrink into nothing by the side of your presence even.'

After their first meeting, when they are alone, Rosa begs Helena to keep her arms round her while they talk of Jasper and to stay with her afterwards. Perhaps the affinity between Helena and Neville is so strong that she shares his attraction towards Rosa; at any rate, she frequently behaves more like a lover than a friend. Having confessed her ignorance and lack of accomplishments to Rosa, she says, 'My pretty one, can I help it? There is a fascination in you!' When Rosa hints that Edwin doesn't feel this fascination very strongly, Helena cries, ' "Why, surely he must love you with all his heart" with an earnestness that threatened to blaze into ferocity if he didn't.' We leave them embraced, like Grace and Marion: 'The lustrous gipsy face drooped over the clinging arms and bosom, and the wild black hair fell down protectingly over the childish form. There was a slumbering gleam of fire in the intense dark eyes, though they were then softened with compassion and admiration.'

Something of this relationship had already been prefigured in *Dombey and Son*, although with a difference. Edith is proud and fierce like Helena, but she is cold and unloving except to Florence, while Helena, for all her strength of will and powers of endurance, is intensely loving. But Edith's devotion to Florence is even more passionate than Helena's for Rosa: 'Was this the woman who now sat beside [Florence] in a carriage, with their arms entwined, and who, while she courted and entreated her to love and trust her, drew her fair head to nestle on her breast, and would have laid down life to shield it from wrong or harm?' The nature of her love, again, is more like that of a lover than of a friend. She spends the night before her wedding by Florence's side, impelled to do so by a mysterious attraction which resembles that of Porphyro to Madeline in *The Eve of St Agnes*:

A light was burning there, and showed her Florence in her bloom of innocence and beauty, fast asleep. Edith held her breath, and felt herself drawn on towards her.

Drawn nearer, nearer, nearer yet; at last, drawn so near, that stooping down, she pressed her lips to the gentle hand that lay outside the bed, and put it softly to her neck. Its touch was like the prophet's rod of old, upon the rock. Her tears sprung forth beneath it, as she sunk upon her knees, and laid her aching head and streaming hair upon the pillow by its side.

Thus Edith Granger passed the night before her bridal. Thus the sun found her on her bridal morning.

Similarly, on the night of her return home from her honeymoon, she takes Florence to her breast 'tenderly and gently' and then puts her to bed. When Florence wakes from a nightmare 'in the grey light of the morning', she hears a soft voice in her ear and returns Edith's caress. We do not know whether she has been with Florence all night, but this is one more stage in Florence's unconscious rivalry with her father for Edith's affections. Yet although Edith would have 'laid down life' to shield Florence, what she cannot lay down is her own pride and the memory of her wrongs; and so it is not she who saves Florence. But Helena was probably destined to save Rosa from Jasper's clutches and bring him to justice.

That there is a strong element of the maternal in Edith's love may be seen from the similarity between her parting with Florence and Lady Dedlock's with Esther. Edith says:

> 'Now, goodbye, my life! . . . These kisses for a blessing on your head! My own dear Florence. my sweet girl, farewell!'
> 'To meet again!' cried Florence.
> 'Never again! Never again! When you leave me in this dark room, think that you have left me in the grave. Remember only that I was once, and that I loved you!'

The style is less melodramatic four years later when Esther says goodbye to her mother, but still there is a resemblance:

> We never could associate, never could communicate, never probably from that time forth could interchange another word, on earth. She put into my hands a letter she had written for my reading only [Edith too gives Florence a letter]; and said, when I had read it, . . . I must evermore consider her as dead. . . . 'My child, my child!' she said. 'For the last time! These kisses for the last time! These arms upon my neck for the last time! We shall meet no more . . . '

Lady Dedlock is, like Edith, a cold, proud, beautiful woman who has, as she says, murdered within her breast 'the only love and truth of which it is capable.' Edith has a dead child and a substitute daughter; Lady Dedlock thinks her child dead and finds a daughter (for a short time) in Rosa. This relationship is of little importance within the plot and is only of interest here because, again, it supersedes a relationship with a lover:' "I don't think you would wish to leave me just yet, Rosa, even for a lover?" "No my Lady! Oh, no!" Rosa looks up, quite frightened at the thought.' And when Mr Rouncewell comes to take Rosa away to her fiancé, 'the weeping girl covers her hand with kisses, and says what shall she do, when they are separated!' Edith hates her husband and Lady Dedlock respects hers, but still her tenderness is reserved for her young protégée rather than for him.

Edith Dombey and Lady Dedlock are not saved from their destinies by the love of Florence and Rosa; but in *Hard Times* Louisa, like them proud and cold and empty-hearted but for one affection, is at least saved from total misery by Sissy, though she is to know only vicarious happiness. The situation is ambiguous because, as so often, Dickens' unconscious mind is driving him against the exigencies of the plot. Louisa has fled of her own accord from Harthouse to her father and has no intention of seeing her would-be seducer again, yet Sissy is definitely presented as her champion against Harthouse and as her saviour. She is the victor and he the vanquished, in a battle which never actually takes place. Dickens stresses that Sissy has come to him of her own accord, not as a messenger from Louisa:

> 'May I be permitted to inquire, if you are charged to convey that information to me in those hopeless words, by the lady of whom we speak?'
> 'I have no charge from her. . . . You must believe that there is no more hope of your ever speaking with her again, than there would be if she had died when she came home last night. . . . I have only the commission of my love for her, and her love for me . . . '

It is evident that Sissy is here the Angel Messenger; she is like Nell rousing her grandfather to flee from temptation ('He looked at her as if she were a spirit') or Martha rescuing Emily ('I am a ghost that calls to her from beside her open grave!').

The loving or maternal figure (the words are synonymous on one level of Dickens' feeling) as redemptorix is particularly connected with fallen women. Nancy, though not saved from a fearful death, is at least spiritually saved by Rose Maylie, as are Lilian Fern by Meg Veck and Alice Marwood by Harriet Carker. Before Emily has herself 'fallen' she helps Martha by giving her money and by accepting her as still human; it is because of this that Martha saves her from a life of degradation. Agnes too, the guardian angel of the book, is associated with Emily by saluting her with a kiss before she sails for her new life in the Antipodes. Agnes, herself untouched by sexuality, is allowed to see Emily's face (transformed, or perhaps made dangerous, by sexual experience) although David may not see it until she is out of reach: 'Then I saw her, at her uncle's side, and trembling on his shoulder. He pointed to us with an eager hand, and she saw us, and waved her last goodbye to me. . . . Surrounded by the rosy light, and standing high upon the deck apart together, . . . they solemnly passed away.'

Dickens' fallen women are always seen either in this apocalyptic light or under the shadow of the darkly falling night – hardly ever in the natural light of day. We tend to think of this blend of romantic horror and romantic pity for the fallen woman as a convention of Victorian literature; but, if it is so, it seems to have been a convention originating with Dickens himself. Mrs Gaskell, George Eliot, Thackeray, Meredith, Hardy, all write of unmarried women with sexual experience, and though they may feel a deeper religious, moral or social condemnation than we should feel now, in none of them is there any of Dickens' mysterious horror. And yet he had more reason than any other novelist to write realistically on this subject, since he was closely involved for over ten years in the running of Angela Burdett Coutts' Home for Homeless Women.* He could, in letters and articles, write with perfect realism about these girls: the Irish girl who, after getting dead drunk, 'used the most horrible language and made a very repulsive exhibition of herself',[2] the girl who was found in the early hours of the morning entertaining a policeman in the kitchen. Why then can no trace of these real girls, or of Dickens' commonsense attitude to them, be found in Alice Brown or Emily or Martha?

---

* The Home was originally intended only for ex-prostitutes, though for lack of suitable applicants it admitted various classes of homeless women. Dickens' *Appeal* was specifically directed, with throbbing rhetoric, to fallen women, many of whom preferred their 'dreadful' life to life in Urania Cottage.

As we have seen in his fictional treatment of mothers and children, wherever a character connects with the themes of his unconscious imagery, that character tends to move from naturalism to myth. What role, then, does the fallen woman play in the theatre of Dickens' imagination? I think it must be that she has been wronged, and wronged in the one way that touched his deepest feelings – she has been loved too little, or loved and abandoned. She represents, then, an aspect of the child rather than of the mother.*

Nancy is what she is because she was 'one of those children born and bred in neglect and vice, who have never known what childhood is'. Fagin, the only father-figure in her life, has used her for his own ends: 'I thieved for you when I was a child . . . the cold wet dirty streets are my home; and you're the wretch that drove me to them long ago, and that'll keep me there, day and night, day and night, till I die!' She is murdered because Bill Sikes too has only been making use of her, although she has loved him. Emily has merely been used by Steerforth for sexual purposes; and Martha must at some time have been abandoned by a lover, since she was at one time employed with Emily at Omer and Joram's and therefore was presumably not driven on to the streets by necessity. (Lilian Fern is an exception; she does become a street-walker because of her desperate poverty, and this in spite of being tenderly loved by Meg.)

Those other nearly-fallen women, Edith Dombey, Annie Strong and Louisa Gradgrind, all have rejecting mothers and all turn from the false refuge of merely sexual love. Edith is saved at least from real guilt by her love for Florence; Annie is saved by her love for her father-surrogate and his for her; Louisa, as Dickens becomes more sure of his theme's direction, is saved by Sissy's tender and protective love, the love that should have come from a mother. Finally Mrs Edson, Jemmy Lirriper's young unmarried mother, abandoned during her pregnancy, is sheltered and loved by a surrogate mother, and here at last the apocalyptic light fades into the ordinary light of day. It is no angel of perfection who takes her in, saves her life and adopts her newborn child; it is a silly gossipping old lodging-house

* And George Watt in his Introduction to *The Fallen Woman in the Nineteenth Century English Novel* points out that at that time 'the fallen woman had no power to assert herself; she had few rights, if any'. She is an aspect of the child in this respect too.

keeper, the last of the line of characters developing from Mrs Nickleby, who was in the beginning Mrs John Dickens.

This, I think, represents a real working-through of a theme. We do not know whether his mother's death in September 1863 helped Dickens to any kind of release from his bitter feelings about her, but it may well be that Mrs Lirriper (whose story was published in the Christmas Number of *All the Year Round* for 1863) is his reconciliation with the mother who had for so many years meant nothing to him.

But those who are wronged usually feel resentment and perhaps desire for revenge. 'Good' Victorian characters did not have these feelings; the desire to revenge herself on Carker makes Alice Marwood a 'bad' character and she is redeemed by ceasing to feel this, in a way that Edith, who still feels bitterness against her husband, cannot be. Dickens has to split these feelings off from the 'good' characters who might be expected to feel them, and so we get a whole range of women who express the other side of the wronged but 'good' ones. Edith Dombey in fact unites both 'good' and 'bad' aspects, and this makes her ambivalent in nature, difficult for her creator to handle and uneasy in effect; yet precisely because the conflicting emotions are not split, she is a more powerful personality than any other woman in Dickens until we come to Helena Landless – that is to say, she has more potential as a whole woman than any of the other female characters.

The relationship between Rosa Dartle and Mrs Steerforth is a picture of what Lady Dedlock and her Rosa might have become if the negative feelings in such a relationship had not been suppressed: 'Rosa, kneeling at her feet, by turns caresses her and quarrels with her'. It is what Miss Wade and Tattycoram always are. This is the love-hate relationship that comes from need and the resentment of need, and it may in part represent the hostility Dickens felt for the women he was so irresistibly drawn to, who could not give him what he craved, any more than the two Rosas and Tattycoram can satisfy their partners.

Besides her dependence on Mrs Steerforth (who, like her son, both makes use of her and is carelessly fond of her) Rosa Dartle also fiercely resents the fatal attraction she has felt for Steerforth. But she resents even more the love that others feel for him, and defends her own love so vehemently that it seems as though she needs to assure herself that she is capable of love and to defend herself from the knowledge that her love is in fact hostile. 'I loved him better than you ever loved him,' she taunts his bereaved mother fiercely. 'I could have loved him and asked no return ... I could have been the slave of his caprices for a word of love a year ... My love would have been devoted – would have trod your petty whimpering under foot!' Yet when she is confronted with a love which has really sacrificed itself, she is beside herself with fury. When Emily says that she trusted and loved Steerforth, 'Rosa Dartle sprang up from her seat; recoiled; and in recoiling struck at her, with a face of such malignity, so darkened and disfigured by passion, that I had almost thrown myself between them.' As her love is hatred, so her hatred is allied to love; she is fascinated by Emily, and irresistibly impelled to torment her.

We are told that Rosa Dartle is a motherless child. Miss Wade is motherless and fatherless, and so is Tattycoram. They are unconsciously drawn together by their need not only to love, but also to hate each other. Miss Wade has always known this need, and suffering has been an essential ingredient of her love. Even as a child it is for her a condition of love that she wound and be wounded:

> When we were left alone in our bedroom at night, I would reproach her with my perfect knowledge of her baseness; and then she would cry and cry and say I was cruel, and then I would hold her in my arms till morning; loving her as much as ever, and often feeling as if, rather than suffer so, I could so hold her in my arms and plunge to the bottom of a river – where I would still hold her after we were both dead.

She has been abandoned by Gowan as Rosa has been abandoned by Steerforth; and their resentment is the more bitter because Steerforth and Gowan are invulnerable. Miss Wade is as eager to see Pet as Rosa was to see Emily: 'I was restlessly curious to look at her – so curious that I felt it to be one of the few sources of entertainment left to me'; and her unconscious source of interest is the same – she wants to see a woman who is really capable of love.

Rosa Dartle and Miss Wade, although they are seen mainly from the outside, are allowed some expression of their emotions from the inside; and what both express is a need so desperate that love itself is synonymous with hostility and suffering. In *Great Expectations* Dickens carries this theme to its logical conclusion. Estella is often spoken of by critics as though she were an innovation among Dickens' heroines: 'Estella does represent a real advance in Dickens' perception of women,' says Angus Wilson; '...we do see, in her resistance to others' management, a recognition of a woman as an individual having her own demands on life.'[3] But this is simply not true. Estella is not a breakaway from the heroines like Agnes and Esther and Little Dorrit; she is the last of the women from Edith Dombey through Rosa Dartle, Lady Dedlock, Louisa Gradgrind, Miss Wade and Mrs Clennam to Mme Defarge and Mrs Joe, women who assert with rage and resentment that children have a *right* to be loved, who show in their own persons that those who are deprived of this right feel frustration, hostility and a despairing void in the heart.

Estella makes no demands at all on life, because she has been so deeply wronged, so hideously damaged, that only by rejecting all emotion, all personal life, can she survive at all. She cannot allow herself to feel the anger or the craving for love that show in Rosa Dartle or Miss Wade, because these feelings would be so overwhelming that they would destroy her, as only one of them destroys Mme Defarge, who has allowed herself to feel nothing but the desire for revenge.

Mrs Clennam suppresses everything but bitterness in herself for many years, and when at last she allows herself to remember, and thus experience again, her craving to be loved by her husband or by Arthur, she is literally paralysed – she never moves or speaks again. Estella is living in this inner paralysis, because this is the only way she can live. She never really speaks or moves; this is why we are shocked at those few moments when she expresses any real feeling, however trivial – when she murmurs 'Wretches!' while passing Newgate and when she laughs 'with real enjoyment' at the thought of Miss Havisham's relatives being discomfited. She must not feel at all; she has, as she herself says, no heart. Those others at least know love as suffering, or at worst as hostility; Estella dares not admit love as feeling at all. 'It seems', she says, 'that there are sentiments, fancies – I don't know how to call them – which I am not able to comprehend. When you say you love me, I know what you mean as a form of words; but nothing more. You address nothing in my breast, you touch nothing there. I don't care for what you say at all . . . '

The psychological truth of Estella is so deep that she must have risen directly from Dickens' unconscious mind. She is the true type of Bruno Bettelheim's *Empty Fortress*; she has perpetually to be on guard, perpetually to fortify herself against feeling in order to exist. This is why she must marry Bentley Drummle, who will never destroy her fortress with the least breath of love. (It is, I think, Bettelheim who says that love is for the empty heart the greatest danger and the deepest fear.) And the fortress is empty indeed: she makes no demands on life because there is nothing that she dares to want, she is a girl without aims, without interests, without motives, without a purpose. We can never see Estella from the inside, because she has no inside: she is hollow like the beautiful ash-tree lady in *Phantastes* and, like her, is fatal to those she attracts.

Her relationship with Miss Havisham is also in the direct line. 'Did I never give her burning love, inseparable from jealousy at all times, and from sharp pain . . . ?' It is Miss Wade who speaks; but it could be Miss Havisham. As Dickens tunnels all the time deeper into the situation, he comes at last to the scene he must face: the deprived child confronts the mother whose love has not been enough. He still cannot face this scene with a real mother; Miss Havisham is only 'mother by adoption'. But the mother who has deprived the child of love is seen for the first time clearly: she has not been able to love enough only because she has been herself rejected, has used the child for her own needs only because those needs were so desperate. All the sympathy in the world cannot change the situation, however, as Estella sees it: 'Mother by adoption, I have said that I owe everything to you. . . . All that you have given me, is at your own command to have again. Beyond that, I have nothing. And if you ask me to give you what you never gave me, my gratitude and duty cannot do impossibilities. . . . I must be taken as I have been made.'

' . . . as I have been made.' Estella cannot help being what she is, any more than Miss Havisham can help having made her what she is. Pip forgives Miss Havisham, but Estella does not. She cannot hate, she cannot love, and so she cannot forgive. *Great Expectations* ends this theme, as it ends others. When Estella appears in a later book, she will be Mrs Wilfer, shorn of her tragedy and her attraction. *Edwin Drood* might have taken it up again, but with a difference: the heroine here might really have been an innovation. Helena has the memory of bitter sorrow and wrong, she is proud and resentful like Lady Dedlock and Edith Dombey and Miss Wade. What Neville says of himself must be true for her too: 'I have had, from my earliest remembrance, to suppress a deadly and bitter hatred. This has made me secret and revengeful . . . This has caused me to be utterly wanting in I don't know what emotions, or remembrances, or good instincts – I have not even a name for the thing, you see!' And yet, unlike Louisa Gradgrind and Estella, who are also 'utterly wanting' in the thing for which they have no name (which is the ability to give love), Helena is going to use the qualities which her sufferings have brought out in her for positive good; she could have been, I believe, an instrument of destruction to the wicked and of salvation to the innocent. If *Edwin Drood* had been completed, we might have seen more than the mere solution of the enigma of its plot.

While it may be true that Dickens can never create a complete woman, yet his women are not mere stereotypes, nor, if we cease to look for naturalistic portraiture, are they as unreal as they are said to be. For it is actually in their lack of wholeness that their claim to reality lies. Each represents some part of woman, split off and made to seem as though it were the whole. They may seem because of this to be stereotypes; but if they do, they are the eternal types that exist in all women: the child, the mother, the saviour, the avenger, the destroyer. All women have these elements within them, as folk-tales have always told: it is the primitive (and therefore the childish) mind which separates them, and the mature mind which is able to see them as parts of a whole. Dickens never saw that whole woman, but his unconscious explorations of the theme that obsessed him were bringing him closer to her. The man who cannot see woman whole cannot see man whole either. If only Dickens had not died when he did! After Helena we might have seen a new character, a real innovation among heroines.

Esther Summerson has been deprived of a childhood. Not only what she is, but *that* she is, her very existence, has been neglected, so that she feels guilty for the crime committed by her mother. This aspect of her story will be discussed more fully in a later chapter, since it is the themes of the split self and the search for the mother with which I am here concerned. Esther might have been like Edith Dombey and Fanny Dorrit and Miss Wade, but she is not. She is the first full-length exploration from inside (though Florence Dombey and Little Dorrit are preliminary studies) of all those rejected children whose maxim is 'If you can't beat 'em, join 'em'.

We never know, because she does not know, what her true self was like: the struggle to suppress it is over before her conscious memories begin. When Esther's story opens, she has already accepted her godmother's version of events and has trained herself never to question them: her godmother is 'good' and she is 'bad'. 'She was so good herself, I thought, that the badness of other people made her frown all her life. I felt so different from her ... so poor, so trifling, and so far off; that I never could be unrestrained with her – no, could never even love her as I wished. It made me very sorry to consider how good she was, and how unworthy of her I was.' She knows that she must be 'bad' because she is rejected; she hopes that it is only because she has done something bad, and feels that her crime must be something to do with her mother. 'What did I do to her?' she asks her godmother, ' ... and why is it my fault?' But she learns that she is not rejected for what she has done, which might be repented of and atoned for, but for what she is, for her very existence; and that she has 'brought no joy, at any time, to anybody's heart'. This is the wound that can never be healed: 'perhaps I might still feel such a wound,' she says, 'if such a wound could be received more than once'; and from that day she decides that if she is not acceptable, she must create a self that will be accepted. 'I would try, as hard as ever I could, to repair the fault I had been born with (of which I confusedly felt guilty and yet innocent) and would strive as I grew up to be industrious, contented, and kind-hearted, and to do some good to some-one, and win some love to myself if I could.'

These two selves are emphasised by Esther's habit of addressing her other self in moments of crisis, as when, going to London in the coach, 'I made myself sob less, and persuaded myself to be quiet by saying very often, "Esther, now, you really must! This *will not* do!" ' Again, before Allan Woodcourt leaves on his long voyage, 'I naturally said, "Esther! You to be low-spirited! *You!*" And it really was time to say so, for I – yes, I really did see myself in the glass, almost crying. "As if you had anything to make you unhappy, instead of everything to make you happy, you ungrateful heart!" said I.' Before she looks in the mirror after her illness, when she takes up housekeeping again at Bleak House, when she leaves Ada with Richard and especially when she has read Mr Jarndyce's proposal of marriage, she has to sustain, as it were, the self she has created.

My eyes were red and swollen, and I said, 'O, Esther, Esther, can that be you!' I am afraid the face in the glass was going to cry again at this reproach, but I held up my finger at it, and it stopped. 'That is more like the composed look you comforted me with, my dear, when you showed me such a change!' said I, beginning to let down my hair. 'When you are mistress of Bleak House, you are to be as cheerful as a bird. In fact, you are always to be cheerful; so let us begin for once and for all.'

But because her determination to 'win some love', to make herself acceptable by being what others want her to be, has led her precisely to this marriage which is to be a complete renunciation of her real wishes, she cannot entirely command her feelings: 'Still I cried very much; not only in the fulness of my heart after reading the letter, not only in the strangeness of the prospect . . . but as if something for which there was no name or distinct idea were indefinitely lost to me. I was very happy, very thankful, very hopeful; but I cried very much.'
It is only in the scene with Lady Dedlock that this habit of addressing herself (which seems coy and tiresome unless the reader accepts its deep psychological truth) disappears without trace. Esther suffers something like a birth herself – 'I looked at her; but I could not see her, I could not hear her, I could not draw my breath. The beating of my heart was so violent, and wild, that I felt as if my life were breaking from me' – but for once she makes no attempt to bring this tumult of emotions into order, nor to feel what she ought to feel: she simply feels. The moment that she knows her mother loves her, she is made whole, able to experience spontaneous agony, despair, love. Her mother's love is made manifest before a word is spoken between them:

I was rendered motionless. Not so much by her hurried gesture of entreaty, not so much by her quick advance and outstretched hands, not so much by the great change in her manner, and the absence of a haughty self-restraint, as by a something in her face that I had pined for and dreamt of when I was a little child; something I had never seen in any face; something I had never seen in hers before.

She is loved by Ada, Jarndyce, Caddy Jellyby, Woodcourt and many others – but she has never seen in their faces what she sees in her mother's. It is what she could never have hoped for, that the one to whom her birth had brought disaster should yet love her, that her mother's voice, 'so unfamiliar and so melancholy', should say, 'My child, my child! ... For the last time! These kisses for the last time! These arms upon my neck ... '.

But because Lady Dedlock will not give herself to her motherhood, but is 'murdering within her breast the only love and truth of which it is capable', Esther must revert to her split self. She reveals her feelings of sorrow and guilt at having been born, and although (once more preoccupied with what will be acceptable to others) she hopes they may not be 'very unnatural or bad', still she is forced to the admission, 'These are the real feelings that I had.' Then comes the marvellous moment when, walking in the dusk under her mother's lighted window, she realises that she is not only Esther, but also the Ghost:

> ... my echoing footsteps brought it suddenly into my mind that there was a dreadful truth in the legend of the Ghost's Walk; that it was I who was to bring calamity on the stately house; and that my warning feet were haunting it even then. Seized with an augmented terror of myself which turned me cold, I ran from myself and everything, retraced the way by which I had come, and never paused until I had gained the lodge gate, and the park lay sullen and black behind me.

Of course Esther's 'real' feelings are intolerable to her, and the next day she begins to think 'how wrong and thankless' they are. They must be seen as in some way unacceptable since, accepted, they might disrupt 'the working of the whole little orderly system of which she is the centre'. Dickens too had attempted to make his life an 'orderly system'; the life of his household was regulated by him in an almost military manner, down to its smallest detail. His children's rooms were inspected every day, even to the contents of the drawers; each boy must use his own hatpeg and no other; a boy brushing his coat in the dining room instead of outside 'never by any chance committed that offence afterwards'.[4]

And yet his obsessive orderliness was constantly broken in upon by bursts of uncontrollable restlessness. He was now forty years old, and although Edgar Johnson says that 'through *David Copperfield* . . . he had achieved some inner catharsis, some coming to terms with himself that left him more at peace',[5] this is borne out neither by his behaviour at this time, nor by his letters to his friends. Forster's statement seems to be more accurate, that 'an unsettled feeling greatly in excess of what was usual in Dickens, more or less observable since his first residence at Boulogne in the summer when he finished *Bleak House*, became of this time almost habitual'.[6]

Esther is the portrait of a child deprived of maternal love who succeeds in doing what Dickens could not do: she suppresses and subdues all her 'real' feelings, and yet is loved and admired by everyone who meets her – but what they love is what she has made herself. What she might have been is gone. She tells us how she felt when she knew at last that she had a mother who loved her, and yet must live separated from her:

> It matters little now how often I recalled the tones of my mother's voice, wondered whether I should ever hear it again as I so longed to do, and thought how strange and desolate it was that it should be so new to me. It matters little that I watched for every public mention of my mother's name; that I passed and re-passed the door of her house in town, loving it, but afraid to look at it; that I once sat in the theatre when my mother was there and saw me, and when we were so wide asunder, before the great company of all degrees, that any link or confidence between us seemed a dream . . . '

But she can only say, of this episode so passionate that it is like a first love, 'It is all, all over.' Her mother has been found only to be lost.

Dickens makes no explicit connection between Esther's loss of her mother and her need to make herself indispensable to everyone she knows. He does not see her creation of the second self as dangerous or disruptive; he approves of it (though unconsciously) as a solution for her difficulties, which were his own. Esther could say to herself, 'how far beyond my deserts I was beloved, and how happy I ought to be. That made me think of all my past life; and that brought me, as it ought to have done before, into a better condition.' But Dickens could not bring himself 'into a better condition', no matter how he tried. Throughout the writing of *Bleak House* and *Hard Times* he felt 'the strangest nervous miseries';[7] Forster refers to 'intervals of unusual impatience and restlessness'[8] and to his 'quite unfounded apprehension of some possible breakdown, of which the end might be at any moment beginning'.[9] Like Esther, he was loved and admired, he was the indispensable centre of a far wider world than hers, yet he could not impose happiness upon himself: 'never at rest, and never satisfied,' he wrote, 'and ever trying after something that is never reached'.[10] Whatever it was that he was seeking, he could not find it as Esther found her happiness, and he turned to a far bleaker exploration of his problem, in the character of Louisa Gradgrind.

Hard Times seems to me more like a sketch for a novel than a novel itself, because so many of the themes that had become important to Dickens by that time are merely hinted at, not explored. Perhaps there were too many of these themes in one short book for him to examine any profoundly, perhaps they are spread over too many characters for him to be able to trace any one of them in any depth. Harthouse could easily be the Clennam–Carton figure with the empty heart; seeking the love he lost, or never found, in childhood; but he is not. His immense boredom must of course indicate a void within, but this side of him is not presented in the book. He is Carton seen from the outside, just as Louisa, whose inner emptiness is to some extent explored, is Estella seen from the inside.

Her father has done his best for his children according to his own lights, he has taken a great deal of care to educate them, but with facts only – and here Dickens' analysis of Louisa's misery becomes ambiguous. At first it is attributed only to the lack of anything to nourish her fancy, and she is referred to in chapter one as having 'a starved imagination', for which the metaphor of fire is again used: 'a light with nothing to rest upon, a fire with nothing to burn'. But this defect insensibly becomes a defect of the heart, not of the mind, and the fire metaphor signifies passion, not intellect.

By chapter fifteen Louisa is saying of herself: 'What are my heart's experiences? . . . The baby-preference that even I have heard of as common among children, has never had its innocent resting-place in my breast. You have been so careful of me, that I never had a child's heart.' But of course this is not true: her 'baby-preference' was very strongly for her brother Tom, whom she loves so devotedly that she will marry Bounderby for his sake, and for lack of whose affection in return she is attracted by Harthouse. She must mean, not that she does not know how to love, but that she has never been loved. Her father, though called 'an affectionate father, after his manner', has evidently never taken the fact of Love into account among his collection of facts, and her mother is a dimmer, more petulant Mrs Nickleby with (apparently) no feelings about her family but that they are a nuisance to her: ' "I wish," whimpered Mrs Gradgrind, . . . discharging her strongest point . . . "yes, I really *do* wish that I had never had a family, and then you would have known what it was to do without me!" '

If Louisa really feels the want, as she says, of books, music and entertainments ('I can't play to you, or sing to you . . . I never see any amusing sights or read any amusing books . . . '), there is nothing to prevent her indulging herself in any of these once she is married to Bounderby. But this is not what she is interested in. Dickens has once more abandoned the 'conscious' theme of this novel, which he described as 'wholly directed against those who see figures and averages, and nothing else', in favour of the themes to which he was compulsively drawn in every book.

Louisa is a child robbed of her childhood because her father does not value children for what they are: he wants them to be something else. He is not, like Mr Murdstone and Mrs Clennam, disguising as duty his hostility and resentment against the child; he does, like Mr Dombey, really think that he is doing his best; but for all that, both fathers subordinate their children to their own ends. 'It has always been my object so to educate you,' Mr Gradgrind says proudly, 'as that you might, while still in your early youth, be (if I may so express myself) almost any age.' And so Louisa has had to try to destroy the self within her that needed love, but has only been able to numb it: under the dead ashes the fire always slumbers, waiting to break out. (Her life until her marriage seems to have been given to 'watching the bright ashes at twilight as they fell into the grate and became extinct'.)

She clearly sees the split in herself and knows its source: 'With a hunger and thirst upon me, father, which have never been for a moment appeased ... I have grown up, battling every inch of my way.... In this strife I have almost repulsed and crushed my better angel into a demon.' Although she tells her father that she does not reproach him, the scene in which she runs from Harthouse to him is a fearful indictment, from her lips, of the rejecting parent – that is, of the parent who appears to the child to reject what the child essentially is and to try to change it: 'it has been my task from infancy', she says, 'to strive against every natural prompting that has arisen in my heart'. She finally rejects her father as he has rejected her. 'He tightened his hold in time to prevent her sinking on the floor, but she cried out in a terrible voice, "I shall die if you hold me! Let me fall upon the ground!" And he laid her down there, and saw the pride of his heart and the triumph of his system, lying, an insensible heap, at his feet.'

Louisa is suffering from a lack of parental love. 'Her remembrances of home and childhood were remembrances of the drying up of every spring and fountain in her young heart as it gushed out. The golden waters were not there. They were flowing for the fertilization of the land where grapes are gathered from thorns, and figs from thistles.' She knows in her agony that Harthouse's self-centred infatuation cannot help her, nor can her father, who is as much a castaway as she herself; she turns desperately to the mother-figure, Sissy Jupe. The scene between them, slight though it is, is full of glances and reflections from other books. It is partly a love scene and partly a scene between mother and child; it remembers Milly and Redlaw in *The Haunted Man*; it is what Miss Wade might have been to Tattycoram if her own heart had not been empty; it could be used almost verbatim as a scene between Eugene Wrayburn and Lizzie Hexam, as he too lies 'cast away' on his bed; it is what might have happened to Bradley Headstone and

John Jasper if Lizzie and Rosa had given them, in their desperate need, what Sissy gave Louisa.

As Louisa feigned to rouse herself and sat up, Sissy retired, so that she stood placidly near the bedside.
'I hope I have not disturbed you. I have come to ask if you would let me stay with you?'
'Why should you stay with me? My sister will miss you. You are everything to her.'
'Am I?' returned Sissy, shaking her head. 'I would be something to you, if I might.'
'What?' said Louisa, almost sternly.
'Whatever you want most, if I could be that. At all events, I would like to try to be as near it as I can. And however far off that may be, I will never tire of trying. Will you let me?' . . .
'May I try?' said Sissy, emboldened to raise her hand to the neck that was insensibly drooping towards her.
Louisa, taking down the hand that would have embraced her in another moment, held it in one of hers, and answered:
'First, Sissy, do you know what I am? I am so proud and hardened, so confused and troubled, so resentful and unjust to everyone and to myself, that everything is stormy, dark, and wicked to me. Does not that repel you?'
'No!'
'I am so unhappy, and all that should have made me otherwise is so laid waste, that if I had been bereft of sense to this hour, and instead of being as learned as you think me, had to begin to acquire the simplest truths, I could not want a guide to peace, contentment, honour, all the good of which I am quite devoid, more abjectly than I do. Does not that repel you?'
'No!'
In the innocence of her brave affection, and the brimming up of her old devoted spirit, the once deserted girl shone like a beautiful light upon the darkness of the other. Louisa raised the hand that it might clasp her neck and join its fellow there. She fell upon her knees, and clinging to this stroller's child looked up at her almost with veneration.
'Forgive me, pity me, help me! Have compassion on my great

need, and let me lay this head of mine upon a loving heart.'

'O lay it here!' cried Sissy. 'Lay it here, my dear.'

Louisa's salvation has come too late for her own happiness. She looks, Like Carton, into futurity and sees that, like him, she is destined only for vicarious happiness; but Dickens' dissatisfaction at this outcome is evident in the final sombre words of *Hard Times*: 'Let them be! We shall sit with lighter bosoms on the hearth, to see the ashes of our fires turn grey and cold.'

5

The Children that we Were are not Lost

The theme of childhood is central to many of Dickens' major works. In *Oliver Twist* and *The Old Curiosity Shop* the main characters are children; large portions of *David Copperfield* and *Great Expectations* are devoted to the childhood of their heroes; in *Dombey and Son, Bleak House, Little Dorrit, Hard Times* and *George Silverman's Explanation* the later events have their source in the childhood of the chief characters. Children appear, in more or less important roles, in *Nicholas Nickleby, A Christmas Carol, The Chimes* and *The Haunted Man*, and in many of his contributions to the Christmas Numbers of *Household Words* and *All the Year Round*: notably *The Child's Story, The School Boy's Story, The Boots* (from *The Holly Tree*), *The Ghost in Master B's Room* (from *The Haunted House*), *Picking up Miss Kimmeens* (from *Tom Tiddler's Ground*), *His Boots* (from *Somebody's Luggage*), *Mrs Lirriper's Lodgings* and *Mrs Lirriper's Legacy, Doctor Marigold's Prescriptions, Barbox Brothers and Co.* and *The Boy at Mugby* (from *Mugby Junction*) and *Holiday Romance*. A good deal of his journalism is devoted to reminiscences of his own childhood or the observation of other children.

There must be a greater volume of writing about children in Dickens than in all the other Victorian novelists put together. Indeed, when I was a child myself I considered him to be a writer for children because he wrote so much about children; certainly he wrote some 'grown-up' books and certainly I did not understand all that he wrote about children, but then neither did I understand everything in *The Princess and the Goblin* or *The Water-Babies*. There is not, I think, any other novelist of whom it would be possible to hold this misconception.

Dickens' preoccupation with childhood no doubt had its roots in the fact that he had never left his own childhood behind – that in his inner self he remained always a child deprived of natural growth by the lack of early parental love. We

83

can see easily enough how often the actual happenings of his own life appear in his writings, but we can only feel intuitively – and never know if we are right – when he is writing, under the guise of fiction, about the inner experiences of his childhood and the feelings which, perhaps unknown to himself, derive from them. His attitude to children, as to so many other subjects, is schizoid: that is to say, what he feels unconsciously is often contradicted by what he thinks he feels, or what he thinks he ought to feel. This is reflected in his work by the appearance of both 'real' children – that is, children observed and described by the conscious mind – and of children who have some mythic quality – that is, who represent some archetype or fantasy in the unconscious.

Dickens' attitude to his own children reflected something of this ambivalence. Certainly he loved them, worked hard for them, took great pains about their education and in every way did his best for them; but he also disliked Catherine's fertility (he seems never to have felt himself to have any responsibility for their regular arrival). When Edward, the last child, was born, he wrote to Angela Burdett Coutts: 'I cannot afford to receive [him] with perfect cordiality, as on the whole I could have dispensed with him.'[1]

A father who has been subjected to maternal deprivation as a child may be expected either to over-identify with his own children, or to be resentful of them because they are experiencing what he never had. It is likely that Dickens felt both these emotions, and also that he reacted against his own parents' carelessness about their children's future by a tremendous anxiety about his own, which led to his early regimentation of their lives. It is to this anxiety that most biographers attribute his eagerness to get them all settled in the world at an early age, but it seems to me that Forster has the kernel of the matter when he says that we cannot tell 'to what extent mere compassion for his own childhood may account for the strange fascination always exerted over him by child-suffering and sorrow'.[2]

It does seem as though he identified easily with young children, but once they had passed the age at which he himself suffered so severely, he found it much more difficult to tolerate them. Forster also says that Dickens 'filled the world with pity for what cruelty, ignorance, or neglect may inflict upon the young'.[3] But it was only when he could feel in some way superior to those who had been so wronged that he himself felt that pity. 'Where the poor and helpless were concerned,' says Una Pope-Hennessy, 'his tenderness of heart was unsurpassed.'[4] Yes; but they must be helpless – that is, they must be *what he was* when he was wronged by 'cruelty, ignorance . . . [and] neglect'.

Here we have the reason for his apparently contradictory attitudes to his children and to the poor, which were not in reality contradictory but perfectly consistent, and the reason for his statement that he was chary of showing his affections to his children 'except when they are very young'.[5] It is the reason, too, why Jo in *Bleak House* has to die: if he were to live and grow up, he would become one of those roughs for whom, although they have been wronged by cruelty and neglect just as Jo has, Dickens has no sympathy at all, precisely because they are not helpless. In what way did the 'girl of seventeen or eighteen . . . flaunting along the streets'[6] differ from Nancy? Yet because she used 'the very worst language possible' to him in the public street, he insisted on her arrest, and when asked 'Do you really wish this girl to be sent to prison?', he 'grimly answered, staring, "If I didn't, why should I take the trouble to come here?"'

But this was the man who had written of the Ragged Schools with an insight far in advance of his age:

> The children in the Jails are almost as common sights to me as my own; but these are worse, for they have not yet arrived there, but are as plainly and as certainly travelling there, as they are to their graves. . . . To find anything within them – who know nothing of affection, care, love, or kindness of any sort – to which it is possible to appeal, is, at first, like a search for the philosopher's stone.[7]

For the children in one situation he could feel compassion; for an identical child in another situation he felt vehement anger and a determination that she should be 'took up' – that her life should be, in fact, what Magwitch's early life was, since the police officer in charge of her case said, 'if she goes to prison, that will be nothing new to *her*'. Yet Dickens evidently means us to feel pity for the young Magwitch and contempt for the stupidity of those who put him in prison for being poor and uneducated. These were, after all, the only things the girl was guilty of: she had not stolen from him nor attacked him, she had only used obscene language which, as Dickens would have been the first to admit in another context, was probably the only kind of language she had had a chance to learn.

What was the source of this singular anomaly of feeling? Forster, in one of his more perceptive moments, has the answer when he says: 'with the very poor and unprosperous ... his childish experiences had made him actually one. They were not his clients whose cause he pleaded with such pathos and humour, and on whose side he got the laughter and tears of all the world, but in some sort his very self'.[8] But in order to win the world over to his side, he had had to create a second self which was precisely *not* feeble, neglected and helpless, but in its very nature had to be firm, authoritarian and in control of every situation. 'I have established ... a regular code of laws for the administration of that Institution,' he wrote to Mrs Brown about the children's cottage at Boulogne. 'The washing arrangements and so forth are conducted on the strict principles of a Man of War. Nothing is allowed to be out of its place. ... I go out in solemn procession ... three times a day on a tour of inspection.'[9]

When any situation got out of control, or when his authority was flouted, he could only resort to processes which, in others, he hated and condemned. When a situation of this sort arose in his own house in the unhappy weeks before and after his separation from Catherine, 'my father was a madman,' said Kate Perugini, 'he did not care a damn what happened to any of us. Nothing could surpass the misery and unhappiness of our home.'[10] Even the little boys were left at their school in Boulogne over the Christmas holidays of 1857.

Incidents in his life seem sometimes to be reflected in his works and vice versa. Did he remember, while writing the sad little scene in *Our Mutual Friend* in which the small John Harmon is sent to a foreign school, his own small boys who had been sent abroad at the tender ages of ten, nine and eight? Did he think of Sydney, his little Ocean Spectre, when in *Our Mutual Friend* he wrote:

> ... he was a child of seven years old. He was going away, all alone and forlorn, to that foreign school ... There was his little scanty travelling clothes upon him. There was his little scanty box outside in the shivering wind ... the tears come

into the child's eyes . . . The poor child clings to her for awhile, as she clings to him, and then . . . he says 'I must go! God bless you!' and for a moment rests his heart against her bosom, and looks up at both of us, as if it was in pain – in agony.

When Dickens' daughters were still young, 'they were promoted to an attic at the top of the house, which he furnished very prettily for them. But . . . these nervous little creatures were not very happy there . . . for inside the room itself was a mysterious trap-door, which caused the little sisters many trembling hours. When their father heard of this he went up to the room and with much difficulty opened this trap-door to show them there was nothing mysterious or frightful about it, and reasoned with them so sensibly and kindly.'[11] Did Dickens remember then Smike's terror in *his* attic room? It was 'a large lonesome room at the top of a house, where there was a trap-door in the ceiling. I have covered my head with the clothes often, not to see it, for it frightened me: a young child with no one near at night.'

It was Dickens the adult, the second self, who, though he remembered the child's terror, thought it could be overcome by 'reasoning'; who wrote, 'If the fixed impression be of an object terrible to the child, it will be (for want of reasoning upon) inseparable from great fear. Force the child at such a time, be Spartan with it, send it into the dark against its will, and you had better murder it.' But Dickens the child knew very well that reason could never overcome any deeply rooted emotion, least of all the terrors of childhood, as he shows in *A Christmas Tree.*

When did that dreadful Mask first look at me? Who put it on, and why was I so frightened that the sight of it is an era in my life? It is not a hideous visage in itself; it is even meant to be droll; why then were its stolid features so intolerable? Surely not because it hid the wearer's face. An apron would have done as much; and though I should have preferred even the apron away, it would not have been absolutely insupportable like the mask . . . Nor was it any satisfaction to be shown the Mask, and see that it was made of paper, or to have it locked up and be assured that no one wore it. The mere recollection of that fixed face, the mere knowledge of its existence anywhere, was sufficient to awake me in the night, all perspiration and horror, with, 'O I know it's coming! O the mask!'*

When the conflict between the two selves is not aroused – that is, when Dickens is merely observing children, so that there is no question of wrong or injustice (and it is significant that his feelings as child or father are identical in this respect: that the child grieves over, and the father resents, an intolerable and unjust burden that has been laid upon him) – he is among the greatest of writers. There is no more accurate observer of real children than Dickens, when he describes the Pocket baby which 'doubled itself up the wrong way over Mrs Pocket's arm, exhibited a pair of knitted shoes and dimpled ankles to the company in lieu of its soft face'; or Peepy dipping Mr Noah's head into the wine glasses and then sucking it; or the delightful Polly in *Mugby Junction* finding it, in anticipation of a visit to the circus, 'indispensable to put down her piece of toast, cross one of her little fat knees over the other, and bring her little fat right hand down into her left hand with a business-like slap'. There is the small boy who puts Barbox Brothers at such a dis-advantage:

> The small but sharp observer had eyed his questioner closely, and had taken his moral measure. He lowered his guard, and rather assumed a tone with him, as having discovered him to be an accustomed person in the art of polite conversation – 'What do you do there – up there in that room, where the open window is? What do you do there?'
> 'Cool,' said the child.
> 'Eh?'
> 'Co-o-ol,' the child repeated in a louder voice, lengthening

* Dickens' acknowledgement of the failure of reason to dispel fear appears in the strange little story *To be Read at Dusk*. The bride (Clara) is terrified by a dream, and the benevolent husband is determined to cure her terror by reason. 'He was all kindness, but he was sensible and firm. He reasoned with her, that to encourage such fancies was to invite melancholy, if not madness.' He forces her to meet the figure whom she fears, and she vanishes 'into infamous oblivion, with the dreadful face beside her that she had seen in her dream': in other words, reason has caused her destruction by her own terror.

out the word with a fixed look and great emphasis, as much as
to say, 'What's the use of your having grown up, if you're such
a donkey as not to understand me?'
'Ah! School, school,' said Barbox Brothers. 'Yes, yes, yes. And
Phoebe teaches you?'
The child nodded.
'Good boy.'
'Tound it out, have you?' said the child.
'Yes, I have found it out. What would you do with twopence, if
I gave it to you?'
'Pend it.'
The knock-down promptitude of this reply leaving him not a
leg to stand on, Barbox Brothers produced the twopence with
great lameness, and withdrew in a state of humiliation.

And there is a child portrait of a frankness not to be found again
in English literature until James Joyce or Dylan Thomas:
'Generally speaking, we may observe that whenever we see a
child intently preoccupied with its nose, to the exclusion of all
other subjects of interest, our mind reverts, in a flash, to
Master Mawls.'
Dickens' feelings about his family, so often expressed in his
letters,* sometimes show through in his work. When Mrs
Tetterby says 'I had no more idea than a child unborn', Mr
Tetterby very much dislikes this figure of speech and begs her,
'Say than the baby, my dear.' Mrs Perch (who is pregnant once
more) 'is low on account of Mr Perch, and tells cook that she
fears he is not so much attached to his home, as he used to be,
when they were only nine in family'. Mr Milvey (with six
children) feels that the kings and queens in the fairy stories who
were always wishing for children might have wished the
opposite if they had been curates. And perhaps Mr and Mrs
Orange have the final word on how parents may feel about
children:

 'I wonder, James dear,' said Mrs Orange, looking up at the
 window, 'whether the precious children are asleep!'

* 'I am so undoubtedly one of the sons of Toil – and fathers of children,' he
wrote to Wilkie Collins on 4 October 1866, 'that I expect to be presently presented with a smock frock, a pair of leather breeches, and a pewter watch, for
having brought up the largest family ever known with the smallest disposition
to do anything for themselves.'

'I don't much care whether they are or not, myself,' said
Mr Orange.
'James dear!'
'You dote upon them, you know,' said Mr Orange. 'That's
another thing.'
'I do,' said Mrs Orange rapturously, 'O, I DO!'
'I don't,' said Mr Orange.
'But I was thinking, James love,' said Mrs Orange, pressing his
arm, 'whether our own dear, good, kind Mrs Lemon would
like them to stay the holidays with her.'
'If she was paid for it, I dare say she would,' said Mr
Orange.
'I adore them, James,' said Mrs Orange, 'but SUPPOSE we
pay her, then!'

But it is very rarely that Dickens can allow his feelings about
his own family to show so openly in his work; and he can only
do it here under a double alias. The narrator of the story is a little
girl, and she is revealing her own feelings about grown-ups.
'You love children,' says Mrs Boffin to Rokesmith, and he
replies, 'I hope everybody does.' 'They ought,' she says, 'but we
don't all of us do what we ought; do us?' It is the mark of a 'good'
character to love children, and in *Oliver Twist* and *The Old
Curiosity Shop* the difference between good and bad characters
is precisely that they love or hate Oliver and Nell. Dick
Swiveller's regeneration begins with his compassion for the
Marchioness; Edith Dombey is saved from a lifelong imputation
of guilt because of her love for Florence; the 'melting' of Bella's
heart begins when, 'tender and very natural', she kneels on the
brick floor to clasp Johnny in her arms; Eugene's new life is symbolised by his desire to see Jenny Wren (by whom he has previously been rather bored) and by her kissing him; Mr The
Englishman and Barbox Brothers, both men who have turned
away from their kind, are brought back to the life of humanity by
contact with and care for a child. Even poor Newman Noggs,
whose interest in the Kenwigs' children is limited to replying,
when asked if the new baby is nice, 'It an't a very nasty one,' has
to be rehabilitated in this unlikely manner at the end of the
book: 'His chief pleasure and delight was in the children, with
whom he was a child himself, and master of the revels. The little
people could do nothing without dear Newman Noggs.'

Evil or distorted characters are often sterile (and perhaps this is why Quilp and Sally Brass are not, finally, the parents of the Marchioness); but when good characters are childless they turn outwards to the children of others. 'For poor neglected children, my little child pleads as if it were alive,' says Milly Swidger. 'O why were you never a mother, when there are such mothers as there are!' says the poor girl Caroline to Mrs Lirriper. The change in Redlaw's heart is shown first by his looking 'with compassion and a fellow-feeling' at the pauper child, and finally by his entreating the student and his girl to be his children. Mrs Boffin tries to adopt Johnny, and after his death has Sloppy educated and trained to a craft. Barbox Brothers takes Polly and Phoebe 'into the solitary firm'. Even those who have children of their own become parents to the children of others. Little Dorrit gives 'a mother's care' to her sister's neglected children, and Esther says of Ada's child, 'I call him my Richard. But he says that he has two mammas, and I am one.'

The birth of a child, the symbol of regeneration, is – surprisingly for a writer so preoccupied with the theme of childhood – not very much in evidence. Mr Dombey's grand-children offer him a chance to redeem his errors, and perhaps Joe's little boy will be a Pip with different expectations from those of his predecessor. Richard Carstone's son comes to comfort his young widowed mother and perhaps to 'begin' the world his father failed in. But on the whole the babies that are not mere burdens like Johnny Tetterby's Moloch are mere toys, like that of Dot Peerybingle, 'a very doll of a baby', and Bella's, which reminded her father of the days when she had a pet doll and used to talk to it as she carried it about.

It is not birth which has any mystical or symbolic significance for Dickens, but childhood; and it is especially a source of innocence for those who are guilty (often guilty only of the sin of growing up). The child is often seen as an advocate for mercy or, more strangely, as the future judge of present actions. The child Lucy in *The Wreck of the Golden Mary* becomes a kind of symbol for the survivors of the wreck. Even before the ship sinks she is in some undefined way associated with its safety; and afterwards she is held up to the crew of the second lifeboat as 'the best and brightest sight they had to share'. When she dies, called the Golden Lucy, she is 'buried in the grave of the *Golden Mary*'.

Yet the child may also represent the whole of humanity, since every human being was once a child; and the death of childhood is an event of importance in human life. When Dylan Thomas, in *Return Journey*, searches for the child who was once himself and asks the Park-keeper 'What has become of him now?' he gets the answer: 'Dead.' Dickens feels this about his childhood too: when he revisits the town where he was a child and meets a friend of those days he says, 'We spoke of our old selves as though they were dead and gone, and indeed they were.' And in *The Haunted House* he says wistfully of the ghost of his childhood: 'Many a time have I pursued the phantom – never with this man's stride of mine to come up with it, never with these man's hands of mine to touch it, never more to this man's heart of mine to hold it in its purity.'

Childhood is seen not as one part of a continuous life, but as a separate episode which produces a separate personality, whose life ends as the adult's life begins. But the child, being dead, yet liveth. 'We were all of us children once,' says the Captain of the *Golden Mary.* ' . . . The children that we once were are not lost to the great knowledge of our Creator. Those innocent creatures will appear with us before Him, and plead for us . . . The purest part of our lives will not desert us at the pass to which all of us here present are gliding. What we were then will be as much in existence before Him as what we are now.'

So, the child being 'pure' as the adult is not (and I do not think that there is as much sexual connotation in the word as might be supposed; I believe Dickens means to emphasise the child's simplicity or wholeness compared with the adult's complexity), it is not surprising that the child may be often seen as judge or vicarious justification or even redeemer. When Ada is expecting her child, she says, 'I look forward a little while, and I don't know what great aid may come to me. When Richard turns his eyes upon me then, there may be something lying on my breast more eloquent than I have been, with greater power than mine to show him his true course, and win him back.' Louisa sees 'happy Sissy's happy children' in her picture of what is to be. Carton, also looking into the future, thinks:

> I see that child who lay upon her bosom and who bore my name, a man, winning his way up in that path of life which once was mine. . . . I see him, foremost of just judges and

honoured men, bringing a boy of my name, with a forehead that I know and golden hair ... to this place ... and I hear him tell the child my story, with a tender and a faltering voice.

Pip, in danger of death from Orlick's violence, wonders naturally enough what Provis and Herbert will think of his apparent betrayal of them, and how Joe and Biddy will account for his disappearance; but then he says: 'The death close before me was terrible, but far more terrible than death was the dread of being misremembered after death. And so quick were my thoughts, that I saw myself despised by unborn generations – Estella's children, and their children ... '.

It is possible, though unlikely, that Carton might think of the children and grandchildren of the girl he loves, the more so since in the union of his own name and Lucie's golden hair he may see the marriage that was denied him; but what are we to make of Pip's reference to Estella's children and grandchildren? How should they ever hear of his death, and why should they despise him if they did? He has been of no importance in her life; she looks at him 'unmoved' and 'merely with incredulous wonder' when his love for her pours out 'like blood from an inward wound'. Why then should she ever mention him or his disappearance to her children? No; when Dickens in his writing reaches that intensity of experience at which the inward wound begins to bleed, the image of childhood comes into his mind.

This image, of innocent childhood, is what Edith Dombey presents in her indictment of Carker and her husband: 'How many times have you laid bare my wound of love for that sweet, injured girl, and lacerated it?' She says that if the memory of Florence's wrongs (not her own) could be effaced, the wrong she has done and suffered could be undone. When Mr Dombey is thinking of killing himself it is Florence as a child that he remembers: 'a figure childish itself, but carrying a child, and singing as it went'. During the night of Redlaw's crisis, his only companion is the boy who has never known love. When Pip leaves Satis House for the last time, it is not of his recent parting with Estella that he thinks, but of his childish association with the ruined garden. 'I went all round it, round by the corner where Herbert and I had fought our battle, and by the paths which Estella and I had walked. So cold, so lonely, so dreary all.'

Again and again, intensity of feeling is associated with the image of childhood. Dickens' own childhood had been full of anxiety, uncertainty and pain; his references to this time in his journalism nearly always show this (though often so wittily as to conceal it). In the splendid pieces *Nurses' Stories* and *A Christmas Tree*, it is remarkable what a sense of oppression comes through the apparent lightness of treatment. *A Christmas Tree* begins and ends with 'bright merriment, and song, and dance, and cheerfulness', which 'cast no gloomy shadow'. But among the toys which Dickens recollects from his own early Christmasses are:

> the Tumbler with his hands in his pockets who . . . persisted in rolling his fat body about, until he rolled himself still, and brought those lobster eyes of his to bear upon me – when I affected to laugh very much, but in my heart of hearts was extremely doubtful of him. Close beside him is that infernal snuff-box, out of which there sprang a demoniacal Councillor in a black gown, with an obnoxious head of hair and a red cloth mouth, wide open, who was not to be endured on any terms, but could not be put away either, for he used suddenly, in a highly magnified state, to fly out of mammoth snuff-boxes in dreams, when least expected. Nor is the frog with cobbler's-wax on his tail far off; for there was no knowing where he wouldn't jump; and when he flew over the candle, and came upon one's hand with that spotted back – red on a green ground – he was horrible.

Then there was the 'cardboard man, who used to be hung against the wall and pulled by a string; there was a sinister expression in that nose of his; and when he got his legs round his neck (which he very often did) he was ghastly, and not a creature to be alone with'.

The mere recollection of the 'dreadful Mask' woke him in the night, 'all perspiration and horror' – only one, evidently, of his frequent nightmares, since another recurrent one is also described:

> It is so exceedingly indistinct, that I don't know why it's frightful – but I know it is. I can only make out that it is an

immense array of shapeless things, which appear to be planted on a vast exaggeration of the lazy-tongs that used to bear the toy soldiers, and to be slowly coming close to my eyes, and receding to an immeasurable distance. When it comes closest, it is worst. In connection with it, I descry remembrances of winter nights, incredibly long; of being sent early to bed, as a punishment for some small offence, and waking in two hours, with a sensation of having been asleep two nights; of the leaden hopelessness of morning ever dawning; and the oppression of a weight of remorse.

These are strangely dark recollections of Christmas, and *Nurses' Stories* too, though it begins agreeably enough with pleasant tales, soon descends into the darkness of a child's terror. He remembers the nurse who took 'a Ghoulish pleasure in terrifying me to the utmost confines of my reason'. 'I sometimes used to plead I thought I was hardly strong enough and old enough to hear the story again just yet. But, she never spared me one word of it . . . Here, I always became exceedingly faint, and would have asked for water, but that I was speechless . . . I perceived there was no hope, and resigned myself to this zoological phenomenon' – a black dog 'gradually rising on its hind legs and swelling into the semblance of some quadruped greatly surpassing a hippopotamus' – 'as one of my pursuers.'

Recollections of childish distress seem to pour from him with unusual force and clarity, as in *Lying Awake*:

It is a figure that I once saw, just after dark, chalked upon a door in a little back lane near a country church – my first church. How young a child I may have been at the time I don't know, but it horrified me so intensely . . . that it is still vaguely alarming to me to recall (as I have often done before, lying awake) the running home, the looking behind, the horror, of its following me . . .

Naturally enough, the children of his mind have overcast childhoods too. It is as difficult to find a happy child in Dickens' writings as it is to find a good mother. Mrs Cratchit, Mrs Bagnet, Mrs Tetterby perhaps come in the latter category, and who in the former? The Artful Dodger, Jemmy Lirriper, Polly Trencham?

These three are all characterised by a charming self-confidence, a complete assurance that other people find them delightful and that they can hold their own in any circumstances. But apart from these, Dickens' children have an early experience of sorrow and anxiety – even if the anxiety is expressed in comic form. The semi-fictional child in *The Haunted House* is 'reduced to the utmost wretchedness' by the responsibilities of his infant Seraglio:

> And now it was, at the full height of enjoyment of my bliss, that I became heavily troubled. I began to think of my mother, and what she would say to my taking home at Midsummer eight of the most beautiful of the daughters of men, but all unexpected. I thought of the number of beds we made up at our house, of my father's income, and of the baker; and my despondency redoubled.

Little Harry Walmers in *The Holly Tree* is betrayed by the man he thinks his friend and is separated from the child he loves (whose love has anyway begun to weaken). The children at the beginning of *Holiday Romance* find themselves in an intolerable situation: they are not taken seriously by the adults who are in charge of them, 'those grown-up people who won't help us out as they ought, and who understand us so badly'. And yet, this paradox exists: everything that Dickens says in particular about childhood is shadowed and sombre, but when he speaks of childhood in the abstract, he is Adam yearning for his lost Paradise. 'Ah me, ah me!' he laments at the end of *The Haunted House*, 'No other ghost has haunted the boy's room . . . than the ghost of my own childhood, the ghost of my own innocence, the ghost of my own airy belief.'

Those who have suffered some trauma in childhood commonly feel this yearning for the past, either because they unconsciously hold the memory of an early pre-traumatic period, or because the conscious memory is so painful that it is unacceptable and another memory must be substituted in which the pain at the loss of what is precious and tender becomes more tolerable than the true pain. We have seen that Dickens makes the same split in his attitude to motherhood. Regarded generally, it will call forth such declamations as 'Pride is one of the seven deadly sins; but it cannot be the pride of a mother in her children, for that is a compound of two cardinal virtues – faith and hope.' Yet most of the mothers he writes about fail their children in some way. He is intensely aware of the helplessness of children when adults exploit or neglect them; but I think his presentation of children betrayed by those who love them is totally unconscious. David is certainly unaware of how completely he has been betrayed by his mother, and probably Dickens is too. Yet the recurrence of this theme shows its importance to him.

Those who should care for the child often expose it to suffering because they are ignorant of the consequences of their acts, or because they mistakenly think they are acting for its good, or because they put their own comfort first. Mr Sowerberry, although kindly disposed towards Oliver, beats him brutally enough to satisfy the wife whom he fears. Nell's grandfather loses his livelihood, then drives her from the relative security of Mrs Jarley's in his self-defeating anxiety to get money for her, and finally helps to cause her death by exposure to hardship and poverty. Paul Dombey's poor health is caused by his sudden weaning, and this is Polly Toole's fault as much as Mr Dombey's. She has after all accepted her employer's condition that she shall not see her own family, and she does really put both Paul and Florence at risk, however fond she may be of them. And what of her own six-month baby, left to be brought up by hand in an age when any child not breast-fed was very likely to die in its first year?

Phoebe, Lamps's daughter, is condemned to be an invalid for life because her mother dropped her while in a fit; 'and as she had never mentioned . . . that she *was* subject to fits, they couldn't be guarded against'. Esther Summerson is robbed of her birthright by her aunt, Little Dorrit of her childhood by her father. Johnny in *Our Mutual Friend* is sentenced to death because his great-grandmother is too ignorant to know that he could have been cured: 'to catch up in her arms the sick child who was dear to her, and hide it as if it were a criminal, and keep off all ministration but such as her own ignorant tenderness and patience could supply, had become this woman's idea of maternal love, fidelity and duty'.

Nor does Joe Gargery's love, tender though it is, save Pip from his sister's cruelty. 'You and me is always friends,' he says, 'and I'd be the last to tell on you any time!' But this is exactly

what he does do, about the bread and butter that Pip has hidden,
and Pip is punished. Worst of all, his excuses for allowing Pip to
be beaten simply do not pass muster: 'I'm dead afeard of going
wrong in the way of not doing what's right by a woman, and I'd
far rather of the two go wrong the t'other way, and be a little ill-
convenienced myself.' But it is not Joe who is 'ill-convenienced',
it is Pip who is beaten. Similarly, Dr Marigold's little Sophy is
subjected to such savage beatings that after her death he says,
'It's quite astonishing to me now that I didn't go tearing mad
when I used to see her run from her mother before the cart, and
her mother catch her by [the] hair, and pull her down by it, and
beat her.' And yet when his wife 'bangs herself about', he stops
her simply by holding her. Why do these strong men allow their
children to suffer when there is no need? Why did John Dickens
send his delicate little son to work in a factory when his income
was over £300 a year?

Children have a right to love and security and the right to
grow through each stage of childhood nourished by what they
need for that stage. But although there are here and there in
Dickens the roguish eyes, rosy laughing faces and dancing feet
of conventional Victorian childhood, these are mere decorative
borders. His books are full of children anxious, care-worn,
neglected, beaten, stunted by false love and maimed for lack of
the true love that is their right; and among the most important of
these are the children who die.

It has been accepted unquestioningly by most critics that the
death of Little Nell was a direct result of Dickens' grief at the
death of Mary Hogarth. The origin of this fallacy (as I believe it
to be) is to be found in the letter quoted by Forster in which
Dickens describes his reluctance to begin, and difficulty in com-
pleting, the part which was to end Nell's life:

> I am the wretchedest of the wretched. It casts the most
> horrible shadow upon me, and it is as much as I can do to
> keep moving at all. I tremble to approach the place. . . . I
> shan't recover it for a long, long time. Nobody will miss her
> like I shall. It is such a very painful thing to me, that I really
> cannot express my sorrow. Old wounds bleed afresh when I
> only think of the way of doing it; what the actual doing it will
> be, God knows. . . . Dear Mary died yesterday when I think of
> this sad story.[12]

The juxtaposition of the phrase 'old wounds' and 'dear Mary' has led biographers and critics to assume that they refer to the same thing. I have never thought so. I think that the 'wounds' (and surely it is rather strange that he should use the plural if he were referring to one death?) were much older than his bereavement, which had occurred little more than three years before. Both deaths touched the same old wounds in his heart and thus caused him to associate them in his mind; but the death of Nell is no mere 'writing-out' of his own feelings about Mary's death. That had already been done in chapter 33 of *Oliver Twist*, where Rose Maylie suddenly and unaccountably falls ill and almost dies, for no other reason than to allow Dickens to pour out the sorrow and anxiety he must have felt in those hours before Mary died:

> What had been the fervency of all the prayers he had ever uttered, compared with those he poured forth now, in the agony and passion of his supplication for the life and health of the gentle creature, who was tottering on the deep grave's verge!
>   Oh! – the suspense, the fearful, acute suspense of standing idly by while the life of one we dearly love, is trembling in the balance! Oh! the racking thoughts that crowd upon the mind, and make the heart beat violently, and the breath come thick, by the force of the images they conjure up before it; the desperate anxiety *to be doing something* to relieve the pain, or lessen the danger, which we have no power to alleviate; the sinking of soul and spirit . . .

That is Dickens exorcising a conscious memory; the death of Nell is something very different.

For one thing, although – in an effort to justify what must have seemed to many of his friends his excessive grief at the death of a sister-in-law – he described his feelings as 'the fondest father's pride', it is very evident that his emotions were much more like those of a lover. He showed no such despairing grief at the death of those of his children whom he survived. He regarded Mary as nubile, and she was probably the prototype of Rose Maylie, Kate Nickleby and Madeline Bray, those angels in human form, to describe one of whom is to describe all: 'The younger lady was in the lovely bloom and springtime of womanhood: at that age, when, if ever angels be for God's good purposes enthroned in mortal forms, they may be, without impiety, supposed to abide in such as hers. She was not past seventeen. Cast in so slight and exquisite a mould; so mild and gentle; so pure and beautiful; . . . '.

But Nell is before everything a child: in the first chapter of *The Old Curiosity Shop* her childishness is continually emphasised by references to 'the little creature', 'a pretty little girl'. Indeed it is a surprise to us to learn in a later chapter that she is almost fourteen. That Dickens wanted his readers to think of her in this way rather than as a young girl is shown by his objection to the first illustration (that of Nell asleep) that 'the figure on the bed is not sufficiently *childish*'.[13] He referred to the book as 'the little child-story'.[14]

Nor was it his original intention, as it probably would have been had he still needed to express his feelings about Mary's death, that Nell should die as a necessary part of the plot. We do not know how true it is that Forster first suggested she should die, but Dickens' letters while he was writing the first part show that he at least did not have the idea of killing her off until he was about half-way through. All this is summed up very effectively by the editors of the *Letters* in their preface to Volume II.

> They [the letters] provide no evidence that his thoughts, during the first seventy chapters, ever turned to his dead sister-in-law Mary Hogarth. Nell's creation had been haphazard; her death had been no part of a plan until Forster suggested it: it was as 'the child' that she had pursued him all night after he had written the chapter first foreshadowing her death. . . . He had refused several invitations . . . because 'I am afraid of disturbing the state I have been trying to get into, and having to fetch it all back again.' That 'state' was plainly connected with his grief for Mary, but the suggestion here that it was deliberately induced is evidence against an emotional obsession.

That Nell is both more and less than human, Dickens himself acknowledges at the end of chapter 1: 'So very young, so spiritual, so slight and fairy-like a creature . . . She seemed to exist in a kind of allegory . . . '.At first he makes token concessions to her humanity, in that she bursts into a hearty laugh, gets blisters on her feet and eats stew and drinks ale, but it does not take long for her to revert to her true status. A bird leads the way for her into a wood, she becomes an angel or a fairy guide for her grandfather: 'she bounded on before, printing her tiny footsteps in the moss, which rose elastic from so light a pressure and gave it back as mirrors throw off breath; and thus she lured the old man on, with many a backward look and merry beck . . . '.

This insubstantiality is emphasised by her grandfather's words after her death: 'I often tried to track the way she had gone, but her small footstep left no print upon the dewy ground to guide me.' To save her grandfather from the gamblers she becomes an 'angel messenger', elevated and inspired by 'a new feeling within her', while the old man seems to 'crouch before her, and to shrink and cower down as if in the presence of some superior creature', and looks at her 'as if she were a spirit – she might have been for all the look of earth she had . . . '.

She never reverts to being merely a child. She remains a guardian angel, leading 'her sacred charge further from guilt and shame'. Kit says, 'I have been used . . . to talk and think of her, almost as if she was an angel . . . '. After her death, her grandfather says, 'Angel hands have strewn the ground deep with snow, that the lightest footstep may be lighter yet, and the very birds are dead, that they may not wake her. . . . They never flew from her!' Finally Dickens himself joins in the accounts of her apotheosis: 'she seemed a creature fresh from the hand of God, and waiting for the breath of life . . . And still her former self lay there, unaltered in this change; . . . So shall we know the angels in their majesty, after death . . . A whisper went about that she had seen and talked with angels; and when they called to mind how she had looked, and spoken, and her early death, some thought it might be so, indeed.' And at last she attains, like the Madonna, to the dignity of a capital letter for the personal pronoun.

Now it is not generally recognised that the Marchioness is the corporeal aspect of this spiritualisation. It is no accident that she and Nell never meet, as later the split selves are always to do: they *can* never meet, because they are two sides of the same coin. Quilp, Sampson Brass and Dick Swiveller are the only three who move in both worlds, and none of them ever sees Nell again once she has begun her wanderings: that is, once she has begun the process of dehumanisation. The Marchioness is the same age as Nell (since Dick keeps her at school half a dozen years and she is then 'at a moderate guess full nineteen years of age'); she too is a guardian angel, for she prevents Kit's being transported, saves Dick's life and is responsible for his conversion to a steady life. But still she is Nell's antithesis. Although Master Humphrey says vaguely that 'everything was done by the child', it is impossible to imagine Nell scrubbing floors or emptying slops. But the Marchioness really does do everything. 'I do plain cooking,' she says, 'I'm housemaid too. I do all the work of the house.' She is 'a small slipshod child, in a dirty coarse apron and bib', and the illustrations of her, which Dickens supervised with great care, seem intended to show how ugly a child becomes through malnutrition and neglect.

Nell, on the other hand, never becomes dirty or repellent, although she lies down in a pile of ashes after being soaked in the rain: the illustration showing her after a few days of starvation makes her look haggard, certainly, but not ugly. She is helped on every stage of her journey by numbers of people who fall under her spell, until she spends the last months of her life as a sort of local goddess in a shrine, to which all around bring gifts and worship. The Marchioness is completely neglected and friendless until she meets Dick Swiveller. It is easy to see how she might have been destined for such a pathetic death as that of Jo; but it is Nell, who never forms a real self, who dies.

Forster says that Dickens was controlled 'by his fancies' and that 'he never, in any of his books, accomplished what he had wholly preconceived, often as he attempted it'.[15] It seems more likely that it was Dickens' unconscious mind rather than his 'fancies' which was strong enough to turn him again and again from the plots he so carefully devised. When the conscious mind speaks through art, its subject may be anything on earth; when the unconscious speaks, it makes statements about the artist. Nell's life and death are mythopoeic, not naturalistic (and Dickens appears to have involved his readers of that time in his mythos, in a way he could not do with modern readers); so that Nell is probably a creation of the unconscious mind, as the Marchioness is of the conscious.*

---

* Thus showing that although the unconscious may be more revealing or even more accurate than the conscious mind, it is not necessarily the better artist.

What does Nell's life and death tell us about Dickens? The most significant thing about Nell is that she is never allowed to be what she is, simply a child. Master Humphrey comments on this to her grandfather: 'It always grieves me to contemplate the initiation of children into the ways of life when they are scarcely more than infants. It checks their confidence and simplicity . . . and demands that they share our sorrows before they are capable of entering into our enjoyments.' It is not so much that Nell has to assume the practical duties of an adult (which many children of the poor must do, without harm to themselves) but that she must assume adult cares and feelings before she has grown up to them naturally. She is her grandfather's companion and support – he is not hers, as he ought to be – and after his illness she becomes his nurse and guardian. Finally she becomes a divinity, 'the good angel of the race'. She is not *herself*, she has been forced to abandon what she might have been if the demands of others had allowed her to develop into a normal child and woman, and without her true self she must die.

The story of Paul Dombey is a repetition, more clearly stated as the unconscious pressures become stronger, of Nell's story. Paul is never a child to his father: before he is an hour old, Mr Dombey tells the nurse, 'This young gentleman has to accomplish a destiny.' Before he is five years old, he is referred to as 'the future head of my house'. He is never seen by his father as a child with needs and a personality of his own, but only as a part of his father's greatness, 'or, which is the same thing, the greatness of Dombey and son'. The Blimbers see him as one more young plant to be forced in their educational hot-house. Only Toots, who has 'the shrillest of minds', has the wit to recognise that Paul is 'a very small chap' – perhaps because Toots too has been through the same experience: his voice may mature, but his mind never will. (However, Dickens provides for him very happily by giving him a benevolent nurse-wife.) All the adults who should be nurturing Paul are only anxious for him to serve their purposes. No wonder that when he is asked 'Shall we make a man of him?' he can only say 'I had rather be a child' and burst into tears.

As Paul's death approaches, the mythic element begins to supersede the natural. The child becomes conscious that what he is in himself is disturbing to those around him. Miss Blimber's analysis of his character states that he is 'singular . . . in his character and conduct, and that, without presenting anything in either which distinctly calls for reprobation, he is often very unlike other young gentlemen of his age'. Paul is told that this knowledge will be painful to his father, and 'it is naturally painful to us,' Miss Blimber says, 'for we can't like you, you know, Dombey, as well as we could wish'. Dickens may well say: 'She touched the child upon a tender point.' This is the vital point of any child's existence, that his self should be loved and appreciated for what it is: if it is not loved, the self withers and dies. Florence, his second self, lives on, in the terrible vain quest for a parent's love or even acceptance – vain, that is, until the book's eucatastrophe, the happy ending which may happen in literature but rarely does in life.

It might be argued that the death of Dora scarcely comes within the scope of this chapter. But Dora, whatever her age, is always a child, and is always so treated by Dickens. Among his children forced to be something other than they might have been, Dora is the little blossom that never ripens into fruit. Those others have been forced early into adulthood; Dora has been stunted and forced to remain a child. Although Dickens pities his children too quickly old, Nell and Charley and Jenny Wren, he still seems to approve their early experience as character-forming; but there is a gentleness in his account of Dora's resistance to David's attempt to make her grow up which is explicable only if she is a child. If she is an adult, then David has a perfect right to expect her to 'act a little' for herself and him. But if she is a child, then she has every right to resist a premature maturity.

But there is a secondary aspect to this. In trying to make Dora grow up, David is expressing his dissatisfaction with what she is now. He wants to change her, and Dora reacts as a child would, were any child so articulate: 'You know what a little thing I am, and what I wanted you to call me from the first. If you can't do so, I'm afraid you'll never like me.' The child must be loved first for what it is, not for what it can be made into. And although David answers, 'Why should I seek to change what has been precious to me for so long?', Dora must die, because what she is is not, ultimately, enough for him. We are not present at Nell's death, and Paul's is a little too like the deathbeds in contemporary religious tracts, but Dora's death is Dickens' valediction to all his children who die because they cannot be what they are and live:

'There is a figure... saying in its innocent love and childish beauty, Stop to think of me – turn to look upon the little blossom, as it flutters to the ground!'

Intensity of many kinds of feeling is common in Dickens' novels, but tenderness is rare. It is there in Dora's death; the only comparable moment of tenderness I can think of occurs in *Bleak House*, in the little scene where Charley comes panting home from the washing-tub to spend a few moments with Tom and Emma and tells Mr Jarndyce what five-year-old Tom does during his long day in a fireless room alone with the baby Emma:

'When it comes on dark, the lamps are lighted down in the court, and they show up here quite bright – almost quite bright. Don't they, Tom?'

'Yes, Charley,' said Tom, 'almost quite bright.'

'Then he's as good as gold,' said the little creature – Oh! in such a motherly, womanly way! 'And when Emma's tired, he puts her to bed. And when he's tired, he goes to bed himself. And when I come home and light the candle, and has a bit of supper, he sits up again and has it with me. Don't you, Tom?'

'Oh, yes, Charley,' said Tom. 'That I do!' And either in this glimpse of the great pleasure of his life, or in gratitude and love for Charley, who was all in all to him, he laid his face among the scanty folds of her frock, and passed from laughing into crying.

It was the first time since our entry, that a tear had been shed among these children. The little orphan girl had spoken of their father, and their mother, as if all that sorrow were subdued by the necessity of taking courage, and by her childish importance in being able to work, and by her bustling, busy way. But, now, when Tom cried, although she sat quite tranquil, looking quietly at us, and did not by any movement disturb a hair of the head of either of her little charges, I saw two silent tears fall down her face ...

I think it is no accident that the child here described is named Charley. That other Charley, who at the age of eleven had been in all essentials parentless and had been left to look after his small brothers and sisters, undoubtedly identified himself with all the children in his books whose small shoulders are burdened by adult cares; and the deaths of Nell, Paul and Dora may be in some sense evocations of the death of the childhood of the grieving boy in the blacking factory. But after Dora, these children do not die, although there is every opportunity for Charley to do so when she catches smallpox and indeed, in the case of Jenny Wren, Dickens actually seems at first to be carried away by an old habit. The slanting rows of angels which she sees in the earlier chapters of *Our Mutual Friend* were evidently intended to foreshadow her coming death, as the angels in 'long rows' mark the death of the young sister in *A Child's Dream of a Star*. But Jenny lives to anticipate a happier future with even a prospect of marriage. Jo does die, but I think that is because he is not connected with this theme: he is one of those who 'have no business to be' – and he is, in any case, never referred to as a child. He is probably about the same age as Charley, 'over thirteen', but she is called 'a very little girl', 'the baby who had learned . . . to be a mother', while he is simply 'the boy'.

Nell and Paul begin by being moderately real (Paul was originally meant to 'use' Florence 'as a mere convenience and handle') but the approach of death takes them further from nature and closer to myth. Dora too loses all her natural silliness and pettishness and 'lies smiling on us, and is beautiful, and utters no hasty or complaining word'. These children become perfect as they are to die, and it was perhaps the destruction of what might have been 'perfect' or fulfilled in himself that Dickens grieved over in their deaths. That he felt intense and passionate sorrow when the children of his imagination died is proved by his letters at these times. 'I am, for the time being, nearly dead with work and grief for the loss of my child,'[16] he wrote, after Little Nell's end. 'All the night I have been pursued by the child, and this morning I am unrefreshed and miserable. I don't know what to do with myself.'[17] Similarly, after finishing the number of *Dombey and Son* in which Paul's death occurred, he wrote to Miss Coutts: 'Between ourselves, Paul is dead. He died on Friday night about ten o'clock, and as I had no hope of getting to sleep afterwards I went out and walked about Paris until breakfast next morning.'[18]

But if Dickens is merely working out his feelings for the death of his own childhood, why does he refer to Nell, Paul and Dora as though they had been murdered? 'I am slowly murdering that poor child, and grow wretched over it,' he wrote to Macready in January 1841. (The two chapters describing Nell's death were finished on 12 January 1841.) Again: 'I shall probably not kill [Paul] until the fifth number'[19] and 'Paul I shall slaughter at the end of number five', he wrote in 1846;[20] and in 1850, 'I have still Dora to kill'.[21] Of course any author may speak as though, like God, he can give life or take it away from the characters he has created, but in fact Dickens does not very often speak in this way. He is more likely to say 'I had an idea . . . ' , 'I shaped Mr Merdle out of . . . ' , 'I see the possibility of . . . ' , 'I think I can make a good effect of . . . ' . He tends to speak as though his characters acted in ways of their own as living people do. So it may be of some significance that he speaks of 'killing', 'murdering' and 'slaughtering' Nell and Paul and Dora.

Dickens does seem to have worked through the theme of the death of the child too early old. Consciously or unconsciously, he came to realise that such a child might live and develop and know some sort of happiness. And yet although this theme as such comes to an end, it seems to branch off at a deeper level. When he wrote of Nell, Paul and Dora it would be true to say that he saw them in some measure as being 'killed' by others: Nell by her grandfather, Paul by his father and Dora by her marriage to David. In the real-life death of the self there must be in the child the elements of, if not co-operation, at least submission, so that the process could be said to have elements of suicide as well as murder: 'the tiny self', as Karen Horney says, 'unwittingly takes part'.

It is this theme that begins to appear obsessively in Dickens' last books. In a modern book you could make a child commit suicide or murder; you could not do so in Victorian fiction.* So the theme must move away from the child towards the adult. If a man kills himself, presumably he is in some sense willing to die and therefore does not feel the outrage of murder. How Dickens' unconscious mind, with its usual ingenuity, solved the problem of presenting the theme of the self murdering itself will be the subject of my next chapter.

---

* See Thomas Hardy's two manifestos, *The Profitable Reading of Fiction* and *Candour in English Fiction*. Nevertheless the scandal when *Jude the Obscure* was published (scandal not only because of its sexual implications, but also over its 'attacks' on the 'innocence' of childhood) 'cured' him, as he said, of any desire to write more novels.

6
The Crime of being Born

A sense of guilt was probably a continuous state with most Victorian children. The constant demand that they should never fail either in their duty to God or in their duty of implicit obedience to their parents meant that they must always have been conscious of some degree of failure. This kind of guilt is not explored by Dickens, since it is too much taken for granted, but it is fully documented.

Oliver Twist is subjected to a continual guilt-inducing process from the date of his crime of asking for more gruel, after which the other boys in the workhouse are made to pray 'to be guarded from the sins and vices of Oliver Twist, whom the supplication distinctly set forth to be under the exclusive patronage and protection of the powers of wickedness, and an article direct from the manufactory of the very Devil himself'. Susan Nipper, although devoted to the child Florence, often addresses her in some such way as: 'now, Miss Floy, you come along with me, and don't go hanging back like a naughty wicked child that judgments is no example to, don't!' David Copperfield is perpetually in disgrace with the Murdstones for his poor performance at lessons; Peepy is called 'you naughty Peepy' whatever he does. Johnny Tetterby is the scapegoat for the rest of the family:

> Mr Tetterby having administered the water [to Mrs Tetterby] turned suddenly on the unlucky Johnny (who was full of sympathy) and demanded why he was wallowing there, in gluttony and idleness, instead of coming forward with the baby, that the sight of her might revive his mother. Johnny immediately approached, borne down by its weight; but Mrs Tetterby holding out her hand to signify that she was not in a condition to bear that trying appeal to her feelings, he was interdicted from advancing another inch, on pain of perpetual hatred from all his dearest connections; and accordingly retired to his stool again, and crushed himself as before.

Many Victorian parents were, like Susan Nipper, 'of that school of trainers of the young idea which holds that childhood, like money, must be shaken and rattled and jostled about a good deal to keep it bright'; and many Victorian children were accustomed to being hustled and slapped to a certain degree. David - Copperfield is given orders as though he were a dog, and Pip is 'heavily bumped from behind in the nape of the neck and the small of the back' and his face is 'ignominiously shoved against the kitchen wall' for not answering questions.

Dickens himself seems to have been well used to this kind of treatment – the treatment of children as objects rather than as persons. His description of being 'caught in the palm of a female hand by the crown, . . . and violently scrubbed from the neck to the roots of the hair' resembles Pip's account of his tortures at the hand of his sister: 'my face was squeezed into wooden bowls in sinks, and my head put under taps of water-butts, and I was soaped, and kneaded, and towelled, and thumped, and harrowed and rasped, until I really was quite beside myself'. And the kind of guilt that comes from doing something thought to be wrong was also familiar to him, as we see from a letter to Forster in 1857: 'I feel much as I used to do when I was a small child . . . either with the remorseful consciousness of having kicked Somebody else, or because still Somebody else had hurt my feelings in the course of the day.'[1]

It is interesting that in this letter he connects the simple guilt of commission with another kind of feeling usually induced by the guilt of others. But when a child's feelings are hurt, he is not able to take any external factors into consideration as an adult would do: he feels only that he is not loved as a person. And if he has been conditioned to think that adults are right in all their judgments, he will think that there must be some defect in himself, some reason why he is not loved, and will begin to feel guilt – not because he has done something wrong, but because he is the wrong kind of person. Ultimately he will begin to feel that he is not wanted and that he should never have been born. This is the theme of primal guilt which Dickens explores in so many of his novels.

The characters who embody this theme fall into distinct groups. First we may consider the children who ought not to have been born, since they were wanted by no one. Smike is the earliest of these, a child whose birth jeopardises his parents' hope of an inheritance, whose mother 'never saw him but once or twice, and then by stealth', whose father 'never went near him, to avoid raising suspicion'. He becomes simply an object, for Brooker, for Squeers and finally for his unknown father, and between them his life is broken. It is redeemed from total ruin by his love for Nicholas (who has, significantly, the same name as Smike's father) and by Nicholas' quasi paternal care and protection. But the man who 'in the hot pursuit of his bad ends, has persecuted and hunted down his own child to death' is visited by a fearful retribution.

Smike has been deprived of the right to develop as it were by accident. Although his parents neglected him in his infancy, it was partly through expediency, and his life of misery was unintended; his death is in fact his father's punishment. But there is a long series of characters damaged not only by poverty but by rejection. Hugh, the illegitimate son of Sir John Chester in *Barnaby Rudge*, is the first of these. When he is six his mother is hanged, calling down a curse upon his father; but otherwise his childhood is identical with those of Gill Davis in *The Perils of Certain English Prisoners* and of Abel Magwitch. John Willet describes Hugh's life after his mother's death: 'that chap was then turned loose, and had to mind cows, and frighten birds away, and what not, for a few pence to live on . . . that can't read nor write, and has never had much to do with anything but animals, and has never lived in any way but like the animals he has lived among.'

Gill Davis too has had to frighten birds as a child, and remembers a shepherd ('my father, I wonder?') 'who used to let me lie in a corner of his hut by night . . . and who used to give me so little of his victuals and so much of his staff that I ran away from him – which was what he wanted all along, I expect – to be knocked about the world . . . '. Magwitch first became aware of himself 'down in Essex, a thieving turnips for my living . . . a ragged little creatur as much to be pitied as ever I see.'

The town counterparts of these country children are the child in *The Haunted Man*, 'a baby savage, a young monster, a child who had never been a child', and Jo in *Bleak House*, the 'outlaw with the broom'. They culminate in the figure of George Silverman, 'a small brute to shudder at', 'with no higher feelings than we may suppose to animate a mangy young dog or wolf-cub'. Because these children are unloved, they have no place in the world and so seem as if they had no right to be born. They might all feel, with Jo, that 'it would appear to be perfectly true that I have no business here, or there, or anywhere; and yet to be perplexed by the consideration that I *am* here somehow, too, and everybody overlooked me until I became the creature that I am!'

Dickens may have been trying to convince himself that 'the crime of being born' was a social one and that therefore it could be forgiven, and the innocent little criminal redeemed, by society. He is still suggesting, as late as *Great Expectations*, that society is responsible for Magwitch's condition, as it is for Jo's. But unconsciously he knew that the 'crime' could be one where there were no circumstances of disgrace or poverty to make the child unwanted (although, as we have seen, he found it difficult to admit the possibility of a mother wishing that her child had not been born). In *Our Mutual Friend* he admits that society, even when it does its duty, cannot fill the empty heart. Bradley Headstone has been a pauper boy (like Jo and Magwitch) who has been given the chance of becoming a respectable member of society, with every chance of increasing success; but he throws all this away when he meets Lizzie Hexam. He follows the pattern of David Copperfield, Arthur Clennam and Pip in this doomed love; and for all that society can do, it is love – or the lack of it – that destroys him. And it is love that redeems, in however small a degree, those other lost or brutalised creatures.

In 1884 Dickens wrote *The Chimes*, a story of which the whole theme is, more or less, whether the unwanted have a right to be born. True, the subjects of this inquiry are not children, but the poor. Yet the poor resemble children in many ways: they are helpless and dependent, they have little control over their own lives, they can do nothing to alleviate their miseries, they may be subject to a harsh or an uncomprehendingly benevolent authority and they do not know how to speak in their own defence.

When the story opens Trotty Veck is pondering on this problem in what might be the words of an unwanted child:

I can't make out whether we have any business on the face of the earth, or not. Sometimes I think we must have – a little; and sometimes I think we must be intruding. I get so puzzled

sometimes that I am not even able to make up my mind
whether there is any good at all in us, or whether we are born
bad. We seem to be dreadful things; we seem to give a deal of
trouble . . . supposing it should really be that we have no
right to a New Year – supposing we really *are* intruding – .

Mr Filer answers this supposition very definitely: 'A man may
live to be as old as Methusaleh . . . he can no more hope to
persuade 'em that they have no right or business to be married,
than he can hope to persuade 'em that they have no earthly right
or business to be born. And *that* we know they haven't. We
reduced it to a mathematical certainty long ago!'

Dickens was more disturbed by this story than he had been
since he had killed Little Nell. 'Since I conceived, at the beginning of the second part, what must happen in the third,' he
wrote to Forster, 'I have undergone as much sorrow and agitation as if the thing were real; and have wakened up with it at
night.'[2] When it was finished, he told Forster that he had had
'what women call "a real good cry" '.[3] His restlessness then
became so acute that, although it was November and the
unusually bad weather made travelling difficult, he set off from
Genoa to spend eight days in London, after which he made the
nightmare journey back again. His next full length book was the
study of parental rejection, *Dombey and Son.*

In Florence Dombey, Dickens studies for the first time the
emotional growth of a child who knows herself to be unwanted.
As long as her mother, who loves her, is alive she has no sense of
guilt, but when she realises that her father does not love her, she
begins at once to feel that this must be through some fault of her
own; she is afraid of offending him, not only by doing something he may dislike, but by being what he dislikes. While Paul is
alive Mr Dombey is at least indifferent to her, but after Paul's
death her mere existence becomes in her father's eyes an
offence, a crime. But she cannot accept that her father is simply
rejecting her; she must create a fantasy to explain his apparent
rejection: either he does not realise that she loves him, or there
must be some fault in herself which she can cure and so remove
the obstacle to his loving her. 'She was very young, and had no
mother, and had never learned, by some fault or misfortune,
how to express to him that she loved him. She would be patient,

and would try to gain that art in time, and win him to a better knowledge of his only child.'

In this study of the rejected child's schizoid tendency to lose touch with reality because it is too painful to be borne, Florence's fantasy that her father would love her if she were to die shows the psychological truth of Dickens' art.

> And now Florence began to think, if she were to fall ill, if she were to fade like her dear brother, would he then know that she had loved him, would she then grow dear to him; would he come to her bedside, when she was weak and dim of sight, and take her into his embrace, and cancel all the past? Would he so forgive her, in that changed condition, for not having been able to lay open her childish heart to him?...
>
> Yes, she thought if she were dying, he would relent. She thought that if she lay, serene and not unwilling to depart, upon the bed that was curtained round with recollections of their darling boy, he would be touched home, and would say, 'Dear Florence, live for me, and we will love each other as we might have done, and be as happy as we might have been these many years!' She thought that if she heard such words from him, and had her arms clasped round him, she could answer with a smile, 'It is too late for anything but this: I never could be happier, dear father!' and so leave him, with a blessing on her lips.

This is not only the rejected child's fantasy of being loved and forgiven for the crime of its existence: it is also a revenge fantasy, concealing a wish that the unloving parent should experience the pain of rejection and separation. The punishment of parents is a common theme and it occurs, humorously treated, in all three parts of the *Holiday Romance* very much as it occurs in Kenneth Grahame's *Dream Days*. The youthful narrator of *Dies Irae* wants his relations to be 'made to feel their position first, to see themselves as they really were, and to wish – when it was too late – that they had behaved more properly'. After several variations on this theme, he decides to become a hermit:

> The iron grating was the most necessary feature of all, for I intended that on the other side of it my relations should range

themselves . . . a sad-eyed row, combined in tristful appeal. 'We see our error now,' they would say, 'we were always dull dogs, slow to catch – especially in those akin to us – the finer qualities of soul! We misunderstood you, misappreciated you, and we own up to it. And now – ' 'Alas, my dear friends,' I would strike in here, waving towards them an ascetic hand – one of the emaciated sort, that lets the light shine through at the finger-tips – 'Alas, you come too late! This conduct is fitting and meritorious on your part, and indeed, I always expected it of you sooner or later, but the die is cast, and you may go home again and bewail at your leisure this too tardy repentance of yours. For me, I am vowed and dedicated, and my relations henceforth are austerity and holy works.'

Dickens and Grahame must treat these themes with humour when they treat them openly, because to treat them seriously would be too painful. Florence's desire that her father should be punished must be concealed from herself, and from her creator (though in fact that other victim of rejection, Edith, is allowed to express resentment instead of Florence). What need not be concealed is the unloved child's other fantasy that the past will be cancelled and the parent will be proved to have loved the child from the beginning. For Florence this becomes reality; her father learns to associate her with his beloved lost son: 'He reunited them in his thoughts, and they were never asunder. Oh, that he could have united them in his past love . . . !' She expiates, too, her crime of being born a daughter by giving her father another Paul, and is reborn herself as a Florence this time loved from the first. But she has also succeeded in punishing her father, in fact, since she has won from him the affection of his son and both his wives.

The Christmas Book for 1848, the year in which *Dombey* was finished, was *The Haunted Man*, and shows Dickens still preoccupied with the theme of the unwanted child. Redlaw's obsession with his past is not only conscious but is externalised as a Phantom, an 'animated image of himself dead'. This other self tells the story of Redlaw's life:

I am he, neglected in my youth, and miserably poor, who strove and suffered, and still strove and suffered. . . . No mother's self-denying love, . . . no father's counsel, aided *me....* I was easily an alien from my mother's heart. My parents, at the best, were the sort whose care soon ends, and whose duty is soon done; who cast their offspring loose, early, as birds do theirs.

Redlaw, like Dickens, has experienced an episode of early love slighted and the loss of a 'dear sister' (Mary Hogarth?) who 'lived on to see him famous, and then died'. His past misery haunts him: 'I bear within me a Sorrow and a Wrong. Thus I prey upon myself. Thus, memory is my curse; and, if I could forget my sorrow and my wrong, I would!'

Dickens needed not to forget, but to remember, to bring up into his conscious mind the tragedy of his past. 'Those who do not remember the past are condemned to repeat it', and Dickens at least knows that oblivion of the wrong – offered, with absolute fidelity to psychological truth, by the divided self – is no solution, and rejects it. (Indeed, if a child refuses the memory of its early pain, it may become literally 'autistic'.) Redlaw is 'saved' by the mother-figure Milly, and again it is his other self who tells him that she alone can restore his humanity. His Phantom disappears for ever, but the phantom who haunted Dickens remained. It was at about this time that he wrote the fragment of autobiography that dealt with what he could remember of his own 'sorrow and wrong' and that led to the writing of *David Copperfield*.

We have seen how skilfully he explores in this book the theme of maternal rejection without actually admitting the fact that David's mother is not capable of true maternal love. With equal skill he sets the scene so that the subject is the child's feeling of guilt for existing, without admitting that the child is unwanted by its parents. David feels guilt only in the presence of the unloving Murdstones; and it is Miss Trotwood, not his mother, who 'took offence at the poor dear boy's ever being born at all'. But still David carries the weight that the unwanted child must always bear, 'A monstrous load, a daymare that there was no possibility of breaking in . . . always feeling that there were a knife and fork too many, and that mine; a plate and chair too many, and those mine; a somebody too many, and that I!' His existence has no meaning for himself, and is a burden to others: 'What a blank space I seemed, which everybody overlooked, and yet was in everybody's way . . . !'

Esther Summerson begins her narrative in *Bleak House* at a point identical with this part of David's story, but Dickens comes closer to his theme by creating in Esther a child who really ought not to have been born. Her birth is a disaster: because of it her aunt and Boythorn are separated for ever and her mother, twenty years later, destroys herself. From her earliest years she is forced into consciousness of the crime she has committed: 'I happened to look timidly up from my stitching, across the table, at my godmother, and I saw in her face, looking gloomily at me, "It would have been far better, little Esther, that you had no birthday: that you had never been born."' Esther's godmother does not make her accusation in words, but the child responds as though to a direct statement, and with guilt: 'What did I do to her, dear godmother? How did I lose her? Why am I so different from other children, and why is it my fault?' She feels 'guilty and yet innocent' – how can a child help being born, and yet how can it not feel the guilt of existing only as a burden?

But again Dickens does not face up to the true situation: Esther has not been unwanted by her mother, but in order to contrive this situation his usual skill in scene-setting has to be to a certain extent in abeyance. There is absolutely no reason why Miss Barbary should have concealed the birth of the child from her sister and reared it herself. Still, he does by this means present Esther with a real reason for her feeling of guilt at having been born, since her very existence is dangerous to her mother's reputation; and this gives him a chance to express this feeling openly for the first time.

> I then became heavily sorrowful to think that I had ever been reared. That I felt as if I knew it would have been better and happier for many people if indeed I had never breathed . . . That I was so confused and shaken, as to be possessed by the belief that it was right, and had been intended, that I should die in my birth; and that it was wrong, and not intended, that I should be then alive.

Esther can reason herself out of her misery: 'I saw very well that I could not have been intended to die, or I should never have lived; not to say should never have been reserved for such a happy life', and she can absolve herself of guilt: 'I know I was as innocent of my birth as a queen of hers; and that before my Heavenly Father I should not be punished for birth...'. Dickens' life was, like Esther's, very happy by any external standards, but if his guilt and misery were in any way like hers, he could not reason to such good account as the child of his imagination – or else reason was of no avail. His story for the 1852 Christmas Number of *Household Words* was *The Poor Relation's Story* in which the Poor Relation describes himself as 'only a superfluous something, who feels that he has failed to find any place for himself in the world'.

In *Little Dorrit* his theme is again the child who has no business to be born, and the plot-structure for this theme in some ways resembles that of *Bleak House*. Arthur Clennam, like Esther, has been brought up by a hard, unloving mother-surrogate to whom his birth has been a disaster. By being born he has ruined the lives of his father, his mother and his stepmother, as Esther has ruined her aunt's and ruins her mother's. Again Dickens cannot face the situation of the real mother rejecting her child (although it looks as though she is doing just this until it turns out that Arthur's real mother loved him and only gave him up to the cruel stepmother out of dire necessity).

Arthur's life has been broken by what he believes to be parental rejection; and it is no accident that Miss Wade, that other victim of deprivation, gives her 'history' to him. She recognises the likeness between them, if he does not, though she has chosen a very different way of living with her wretchedness. She forces the world to go on rejecting her, because it is less painful than accepting love, with the possible consequence of loss. Dickens was deeply involved with the episode of Miss Wade and was surprised that Forster did not see its connection with the main plot. 'In Miss Wade,' he wrote, 'I had an idea, which I thought a new one, of making the introduced story so fit into surroundings impossible of separation from the main story, as to make the blood of the book circulate through both. But I can only suppose, from what you say, that I have not exactly succeeded in this.'[4] Many critics have felt, as Forster did, that Miss Wade's 'history' is merely an interpolation, having no more connection with the book as a whole than the stories in *Pickwick*. But it seems likely that to Dickens the themes which he explored with such intensity were always 'the main story', and that Miss

Wade and Tattycoram were both variations on the Clennam theme.

The 1857 Christmas Number of *Household Words* contained *The Perils of Certain English Prisoners* with its central figure Gill Davis, 'a most unhappy man', 'no better than the mud under your foot'. In this story there appears, strangely enough, a Captain Carton who plays the role of Darnay in *A Tale of Two Cities* in that he marries the girl with whom Davis never has a chance. But in 1858 the true Carton appears – 'the only rememberable figure', says Forster, ' . . . the wasted life saved at last by heroic sacrifice'.[5] Carton's life appears to have been wasted mainly by guilt at what he is, although he has good abilities. 'I have no business to be, at all, that I know of', he says; and it is evidently to this feeling that he has no right to exist that he refers when he asks Darnay:

> 'Do you feel, yet, that you belong to this terrestrial scheme again, Mr Darnay?'
> 'I am frightfully confused regarding time and place; but I am so far mended as to feel that.'
> 'It must be an immense satisfaction!'
> He said it bitterly, and filled up his glass again, which was a large one.
> 'As to me, the greatest desire I have, is to forget that I belong to it. It has no good in it for me . . . nor I for it!'

In his preface to *A Tale of Two Cities* Dickens says, 'When I was acting with my children and friends, in Mr Wilkie Collins's drama of *The Frozen Deep*, I first conceived the main idea of this story. A strong desire was upon me then, to embody it in my own person . . . '. There can be no doubt that 'the main idea' to him was the redemption by sacrifice of a wasted life, and that the character with whom he so strongly identified was Carton:

> Waste forces within him, and a desert all around, this man stood still on his way across a silent terrace, and saw for a moment, lying in the wilderness before him, a mirage of honourable ambition, self-denial, and perseverance. In the fair city of this vision, there were airy galleries in which the loves and graces looked upon him, gardens in which the fruits of life hung ripening, waters of Hope that sparkled in his sight. A moment, and it was gone . . .

Dickens more than any man of his time might be said to have lived in this 'fair city' of fulfilled ambitions; and yet, like Carton, he found it only a mirage. It was his own sense of 'a wasted life' that made him so strongly identify with Carton; maybe he too felt that he had 'no business to be, at all'.

At the beginning of *Great Expectations* the theme of the child's guilt at its own existence is again openly stated. Again the plot is so arranged that it is not the true mother who wishes that the child had never been born. It is Pip's sister, and he is continually made to feel guilty not only for having been born, but for everything that his continued existence makes him be and do.

> I think my sister must have had some general idea that I was a young offender whom an Accoucheur Policeman had taken up (on my birthday) and delivered over to her, to be dealt with according to the outraged majesty of the law. I was always treated as if I had insisted on being born, in opposition to the dictates of reason, religion, and morality, and against the dissuading arguments of my best friends.

Pip's birth is not a disaster for others: he is guilty of nothing more than being unwanted. So although he feels guilt, he also knows that it is unjust that he should be made to feel it. His sister, and indeed all the adults round him, force him to behave in such a way that he cannot help feeling guilty, and in this context we have one of those ambiguous situations that reveal so much about Dickens' inability to face up to the true facts. Joe (who really loves Pip) increases his guilt about having told lies: 'lies is lies. Howsoever they come, they didn't ought to come, and they come from the father of lies, and come round to the same. . . . If you can't get to be oncommon through going straight, you'll never get to do it through going crooked.' And yet Joe himself tells some astounding lies to Mrs Joe in order to put her in a less evil temper after his visit to Miss Havisham's. Pip's only comment on this occasion is, 'I have reason to think that Joe's intellects were brightened by the encounter they had passed through, and that on our way to Pumblechook's he invented a subtle and deep design.'

Possibly Dickens intended the reader to infer that the glamour of Satis House corrupted even Joe's simple honesty;

but he is not a writer with much confidence in his readers' ability to make inferences without a good deal of authorial nudging, and he gives no hint that he, any more than Pip, considers Joe otherwise than 'simply faithful' and 'simply right'. All the same he does seem to have some misgivings about Joe's failure to protect Pip from being beaten, since Joe is still excusing himself for this even after Pip's illness, long after Pip has grown up. Again, when Joe visits Pip in Barnard's Inn, Pip takes to himself all the blame for the discomforts of the occasion. But Joe's unnatural behaviour shows him to be as snobbish as Pip. Dickens' distinctions between true and false guilt seem as unclear as those of the adults he condemns.

This situation, where the apparently loving parental figure is inexplicably unable to prevent the child from being cruelly treated, is repeated four years later in *Dr Marigold's Prescriptions* and may represent an attempt on Dickens' part to come to terms with his father's behaviour towards him as a child. John Dickens certainly abandoned his son to the extremest misery and neglect, but he was after all in trouble and anxiety himself at the time. But it is also possible that in his easy-going way he allowed the child Charles to be severely treated by a less indulgent parent or nurse.

The theme of the right to be born occurs only in the early part of *Great Expectations* and then dies away, never to recur. Dickens must have 'worked through' this theme to the point where it ceased to be of importance to him. And indeed we see the change that has taken place in it since the anxiety and uncertainty of *The Chimes*, through the desperation of *Bleak House* to the quiet heartache of *Little Dorrit*. *A Tale of Two Cities* shows the one who 'has no business to be' proving himself of value to his world; and now Pip is ready to take a proper view of the situation. His only crime is that of being unwanted, and he realises that although he has been judged guilty, he is innocent. He accuses his judges of injustice:

> Within myself, I had sustained from my babyhood, a perpetual conflict with injustice. I had known, from the time when I could speak, that my sister, in her capricious and violent coercion, was unjust to me. I had cherished a profound conviction that her bringing me up by hand gave her no right to bring me up by jerks. Through all my

punishments, disgraces, fasts and vigils, and other penitential performances, I had nursed this assurance; and to my communing so much with it, in a solitary and unprotected way, I in great part refer the fact that I was morally timid and very sensitive.

Pip may be, and realise that he has been, damaged by this treatment; but unlike Esther he feels no need to make himself into a different kind of person so that he can 'win' the love he has been denied; nor does he feel, as Clennam does, that it is impossible he should ever be loved. The Accusers become the Accused, and at last Pip achieves a sort of reconciliation with them: 'The times when I was a little helpless creature, and my sister did not spare me, vividly returned. But they returned with a gentle tone upon them. . . . For now, the very breath of the beans and clover whispered to my heart that the day must come when it would be well for my memory that others walking in that sunshine should be softened as they thought of me.'

In *Mrs Lirriper's Lodgings* there seems to me to be a real reconciliation for Dickens, of a more complete kind than Pip's. In this Christmas Number of *All the Year Round* for 1863, a child is born who certainly causes his unmarried mother's death and whose advent probably causes his father to desert her – a possible re-statement of Esther Summerson's story. But no one ever wishes that he had not been born; he is loved from his first moments by a pair of surrogate parents and becomes the centre of their lives. He would in all likelihood never feel guilt, because he is so much loved, but – and again we see Dickens' avoidance of the real situation – the test is never made because the child is not allowed to know the true facts about his birth. It is one of those 'double-bind' situations of whose ambiguities Dickens seems completely unconscious.

Dickens realised that the child who has felt guilt for being born will be damaged. Must this damage be lifelong, or can its victim rehabilitate himself? In 1866, in *Mugby Junction*, Dickens suddenly reverts to a character who is a composite of several earlier figures on this theme. Barbox Brothers is a man who, like Gill Davis and Abel Magwitch, has 'never had a childhood or known a parent'; like Esther Summerson, he has been told that his life has 'a penitential anniversary in it called a birthday'; like Arthur Clennam he has been forced into an employment that he finds oppressive and remembers a mother-figure, 'a hard-lined, thin-lipped, repressive, changeless woman', who is like a blight on his life; like Redlaw he has been betrayed by his best friend and the girl he loved. He is 'travelling from his birthday' and describes his birth as 'a lost beginning', but he finds that by forgiving those who have wronged him, and by taking 'thousands of partners into the solitary firm' (in other words, by trying the well-worn Victorian ploy of doing good to all around him), he can wish himself for the first time 'Many happy returns of the day'.

But Dickens had not found that this kind of loving concern for others could blot out primal guilt, and he is finally driven to acknowledge that the child subjected to this treatment may indeed be permanently damaged. *George Silverman's Explanation* is not particularly interesting as a story, nor is it very good Dickens; Hugh Kingsmill describes it as being 'drenched in self-pity and self-abasement',[6] but at the same time feels it to be an allegory of Dickens' own life. I think it is rather the final statement of the theme that has so obsessed him; and at last it is stated with no imaginative devices to conceal its true nature. The hesitation of its opening – George Silverman makes three attempts to begin his story – shows Dickens' reluctance to face it, and the words in which it does at last open are significant of its content: 'I will come upon it by degrees. The natural manner after all, for God knows that is how it came upon me.'

George Silverman is the child of parents who did not want him and do not love him. (Yet even here Dickens cheats a little: the parents are so poor that a child is an added hardship to their already wretched life.) The father is passive, but the mother is actively cruel, and it is she who makes the child feel guilt – not guilt for being born, but for being subject to those necessities which existence imposes. The whole story is about inexpiable guilt. George Silverman punishes himself by denying himself the greatest necessity of all. He despises the child he has been – that is, he aligns himself with the Accusers – calling him 'a small brute to shudder at', 'a mangy young dog or wolf-cub', 'a young vampire': all animal metaphors which deny the child's right to humanity. He knows that he is innocent but he judges himself guilty, and yet it is the child who sentences the adult to a life without love. It is his punishment – not his expiation, for his is a crime that can never be expiated – to reject the proffered love of the child Sylvia and the woman Adelina, and to act in such a way that his life comes full circle: Lady Fareaway believes him to be what his mother used to call him, 'a worldly devil'. He lives always 'in the shadow', looking on at the sunny side of life, as a prisoner kept in the dark cannot face the light of day. The story ends without hope: 'But my heart did not break, if a broken heart involves death; for I lived through it.' Then nothing lies before him but the churchyard, 'equal resting-place for sound hearts, wounded hearts, and broken hearts'.

It is a strange story to be written by a man at the zenith of his fame, loved and admired by millions all over the world. Yet Dickens said of it, 'I feel as if I had read something (by somebody else) which I shall never get out of my head.'[7] Was the 'somebody else' his own inner self, the self he had tried so hard to suppress? The story ends: 'I pen it for the relief of my own mind, not foreseeing whether it will ever have a reader.'

We do not know whether Dickens was in fact an unwanted child. Perhaps his mother was not a woman of strong maternal feelings; perhaps he was conceived too soon after the birth of her first child. A few hours before his birth she was dancing, in an age when pregnant women were not supposed to exert themselves for fear of a miscarriage. (We remember Mrs Trundle, who being in 'a delicate state of health' had to be told of her sister's approaching marriage through Mr Trundle, 'lest the news should be too much for her'; Scrooge's niece, who has to sit 'in a corner with the footstool' instead of playing blind man's buff; and Mr Toots' solicitude about Susan's 'over-exerting' herself by talking with animation.) But it seems unlikely that this theme would have recurred so often without some cause.

Bruno Bettelheim discovered that many of his schizoid child patients (all of them, in fact, the circumstances of whose birth he was able to investigate) ought not to have been born: that is, each was born at some time of parental crisis, and the birth inevitably caused a deterioration of the situation. Bettelheim felt that the children were aware, even if unconsciously, of these circumstances, and that they were punishing themselves by being autistic (that is, not fully human) for the crime of having been born.

Whatever the root of Dickens' preoccupation with the question of whether unwanted children have nevertheless the right to exist, this is one of the themes that come up again and again in his work. At first the question is whether the unwanted can prove their right to exist by being 'good'. This is what Oliver Twist has to do, and he triumphantly does it. Trotty Veck makes the mistake of thinking that the poor are bad. 'None but the people who were bad at heart, born bad,' he cries, 'who had no business on the earth, could do such deeds'; and he has to learn that 'their Great Creator formed them to enjoy' a rightful share in man's inheritance. From *Dombey* to *Great Expectations* Dickens becomes the defender of the child's innocence and the accuser of those who would deny it a right to existence.

But a declaration of innocence may come too late for the victim of a false accusation. George Silverman acquiesces in his parents' view of himself, and because, being innocent, he has lived as though he were guilty, he must live for ever in the shadows with a wounded or a broken heart. But what of the child who does not entirely acquiesce, who in order to survive builds up a second self?

7

By the Living and by the Dead

In works of fantasy the *Doppelgänger*, or split personality, is a fairly common figure, such as appears in Poe's *William Wilson* or Stevenson's *Dr Jekyll and Mr Hyde*. In his first real exploration of this theme, in *The Haunted Man and the Ghost's Bargain*, Dickens uses the second self merely as teacher, like the ghosts in *A Christmas Carol* and the Goblin of the Bell, whose instructions bring about the existence of a happier (and therefore presumably a more unified) self. Yet the true mythic light glares over the meeting of Redlaw and the Phantom: 'As the gloom and shadow thickened behind him, in that place where it had been gathering so darkly, it took, by slow degrees . . . an awful likeness of himself! Ghastly and cold, colourless in its leaden face and hands, but with his features, and his bright eyes, and his grizzled hair, and dressed in the gloomy shadow of his dress, it came into its terrible appearance of existence, motionless, without a sound.' It is like an 'animated image of himself dead', and its eyes are 'a fixed, unalterable, steady horror', while Redlaw is a man who 'has made too much of all that was and might have been, and too little of what is'. The 'incessant whisper' always in his ears is, 'If I could forget my sorrow and my wrong, I would.' His phantom self gives him this power, and the power to pass on the gift to others; but forgetting the past diminishes the self to the level of the 'baby savage' who has never known love.

The Phantom recounts to him (using the first person) his own wrongs, tempts him to wish for oblivion of the wrongs done to him and shows him the child who has never known love. 'Terrible instructor', Redlaw calls it, and it does indeed direct him to the only source of salvation – the mother-figure Milly. This is technically a perfectly correct solution, since the splitting-off of the self occurs through some defect in the quality of maternal love and it can be healed only by an equivalent love. But when Dickens tackles an almost identical scene eighteen years later in *Mugby Junction* he treats it very differently. Barbox Brothers, like

Redlaw, has lived through a bitter and neglected youth, has lost his only love to his best friend and is also haunted by phantoms – not of himself, but of those who have influenced his life, including his rejecting parent-figures. (Yet while he is conversing with them, he is described as 'speaking to himself'.) By this time Dickens had come up against the 'dead end' of Estella, and the maternal figure appears no more. Instead, Barbox Brothers attempts a quasi parental relationship himself, by 'occasionally borrowing' Polly and by 'brightening Phoebe's life'. It is, psychologically speaking, a distinct step forward, in that the solution is an active rather than a passive one.

Both these Christmas stories are offshoots of Dickens' writing about the split self. In *Prometheus Unbound* Shelley wrote:

> The Magus Zoroaster, my dead child,
> Met his own image, walking in the garden.
> That apparition, sole of men, he saw.
> For know there are two worlds of life and death,
> One which thou beholdest; but the other
> Is underneath the grave, where do inhabit
> The shadows of all forms that think and live
> Till death unite them, and they part no more.

In fantastic fiction a man may meet his own image, but Dickens saw himself as writing (except in some of his Christmas books and stories) realistic fiction. Therefore the parts of the split self must occur as different characters, and it is interesting that they are always connected by death and usually by murder or attempted murder. Shelley's intuition that only death can unite the selves appears to be psychologically correct, though he assumes that only when both selves are dead can they be unified. Shelley may have the weight of metaphysics and philosophy behind him, but Dickens is more useful for the person who wants to become a unified self in this world rather than waiting for the next. He posits that the true self can emerge only through the death of the false self.

This theme assumes real importance only in the last books, after *Great Expectations*. It is as if Dickens, having worked through the themes of the search for the mother and the formation of the second self, is now penetrating to the deepest layers of his unconscious mind. Yet there is a very early groping after this theme in *Martin Chuzzlewit*: the elements which are to become an essential part of it are all there, but jumbled together in confusion, not worked out neatly as they are in the later books. There is a remarkable passage in which, after the murder of Montague Tigg by Jonas Chuzzlewit, it is not the murdered man's ghost that Jonas fears but his own self, that self who has not committed the crime but whom he imagines as having remained in the locked room at his home:

> This made him, in a gloomy, murderous, mad way, not only fearful *for* himself, but *of* himself; for being, as it were, a part of the room: a something supposed to be there, yet missing from it: he invested himself with its mysterious terrors; and when he pictured in his mind the ugly chamber, false and quiet, through the dark hours of two nights; and the tumbled bed, and he not in it, though believed to be; he became in a manner his own ghost and phantom, and was at once the haunted spirit and the haunted man.

It is not an image of himself that Jonas murders, but it *is* a man who has contrived a second self: Montague Tigg, the poverty-stricken hanger-on of Chevy Slyme, has become Tigg Montague, the wealthy President of the Anglo-Bengalese Disinterested Loan and Life-Assurance Company. He is what Jonas would like to be, and he can also make him do what he does not want to do. The ardent and obsessive student of any autobiographical writer may come to feel intuitively that certain incidents in the writings are connected with, or derive directly from, that author's personal life, although there are no facts to substantiate such feelings. I have always felt that Montague's dream after the carriage accident in the storm and Jonas' dream before the murder were in fact dreams of Dickens himself. They have the air of being vividly remembered, rather than invented: the irrelevancies of real dreams invade them, the neatness of invented dreams is wholly absent.

The two dreams are roughly adapted to the state of mind of the fictitious dreamer by the introduction in the first dream of the letter 'J', and in the second dream of Montague's livid head among the crowd. But they can both be validly interpreted as dreams of the buried self, which the dreamer is struggling to repress. Montague dreams of 'a dreadful secret . . . which he

knew and yet did not know, for although he was heavily responsible for it, and a party to it, he was harassed even in his vision by a
distracting uncertainty in reference to its import'. 'Incoherently
sustained' with this dream is another dream which shows the
closed door of his room 'as the hiding-place of an enemy, a
shadow, a phantom' (the word phantom is also used of the
Haunted man's *Doppelgänger*). It is 'the business of his life' (a
strange phrase to use of something as evanescent as a dream)
'to keep the terrible creature closed up, and prevent it from
forcing its way in upon him'. The dream goes on to describe the
horror of the attempt to keep the inner self from breaking
through into consciousness: Montague and his strange helpers
work 'with iron plates and nails to make the door secure', but all
is in vain,

> ... for the nails broke, or changed to soft twigs, or what was
> worse, to worms, between their fingers; the wood of the door
> splintered and crumbled, so that even nails would not remain
> in it; and the iron plates curled up like hot paper. All this time
> the creature on the other side – whether it was the shape of
> man, or beast, he neither knew nor sought to know – was
> gaining on them. But his greatest terror was when the man
> with the bloody smear upon his head demanded of him if he
> knew this creature's name, and said that he would whisper it.
> At this the dreamer fell upon his knees, his whole blood
> thrilling with inexplicable fear, and held his ears.

Jonas' dream seems to take the dreamer *into* the hidden self,
which is seen as 'a strange city, where the names of the streets
were written on the walls in characters quite new to him; which
gave him no suprise or uneasiness, for he remembered in his
dream to have been there before'. Then there is 'a wild hurrying
on to Judgment'; and finally the 'struggling head' of the one he
means to murder rises up among the crowd and denounces him
as 'having appointed that direful day to happen'. These two
dreams are about the hidden self, seen as it were from the inside
and the outside. The first shows the 'constructed' or second self
in terror at the threatened discovery of the real self (as well it
may be, since the existence of the former depends on the sup-
pression of the latter). The second dream is of the inner self

bringing about the destruction of the second self, as it cannot help doing, and thus bringing about the day of judgment.

Dickens' women tend to suppress the second self so strongly that it is never allowed to appear in the real world, as in the case of Little Dorrit, whose real self appears only in a story told to the half-witted Maggie as a 'tiny woman' treasuring a shadow; or as in the case of Esther, where it appears only as a ghost. But there is one scene in which feminine split selves indubitably confront each other, when Edith Dombey and Alice Marwood with their mothers meet on the Brighton Downs. The mythic light shines over the meeting:

> ... there came advancing over a dark ridge before them, two other figures which, in the distance, were so like an exaggerated imitation of their own, that Edith stopped ... The other, in which Edith recognised enough that was like herself to strike her with an unusual feeling, not quite free from fear, came on ... returning her gaze, fixing her shining eyes upon her, undoubtedly presenting something of her own air and stature, and appearing to reciprocate her own thoughts, she felt a chill creep over her, as if the day were darkening, and the wind were colder.

Dickens is not yet in control of his theme, and it dies away. True, Alice does try to save Carker, who has ruined her and plotted Edith's ruin, but ineffectually: Carker has already left Dijon before any warning message can reach him. There is no further confrontation between Alice and Edith, and the resemblance between them is explained away by their being cousins. But that strange meeting stands like a menhir, pointing to the future.

When Dickens can confront the idea of the two selves openly, even in a fantasy as he does in *The Haunted Man* and in *The Poor Relation's Story*, he does not need to introduce the theme of murder because the existence of the inner self is consciously acknowledged. But where the existence of the two selves is expressed only metaphorically or is actually represented by separate characters, the idea of murder, in some form, is always present. Thus the split in Lady Dedlock's personality is expressed semantically, not actually: that is, we are shown that she has a softer side to her nature which she has to suppress except when she is with Esther (or with Rosa, but Rosa is only a substitute daughter). But she is still associated with murder: when she is called Murderess it is a true accusation, only it is not for Tulkinghorn's murder that she must die, but for the murder of her true self.

It has been suggested that Steerforth is David Copperfield's other self: the fully sexual adult male, able to ignore his mother's demands, that David can never allow himself to be. I do not myself think that Dickens even unconsciously makes this identification; but if he does, then my thesis holds true, since Steerforth by his recklessness kills not only himself but also Ham (who could be, if we are using this sort of construction, the noble and self-denying side of Steerforth's nature). This unity of opposites is also supposed by Julian Moynihan to be present in *Great Expectations* in the 'complex unity Pip–Orlick'.[1] Orlick is seen as a double, *alter ego* and dark mirror image to Pip. Professor Daleski does not think that there is sufficient evidence for this identification,[2] and I think that this is simply not Dickens' way of handling the double-self theme; but if it should be a true interpretation, then again the murder motif is introduced.

The first true appearance of the double self seems to me to occur in *The Story of Richard Doubledick* (1854). The title conveys the theme: the hero, whose Christian name is Richard, drops his own surname and becomes Doubledick. He is the prototype of Dr Manette, John Harmon, Eugene Wrayburn, George Vendale and (perhaps) Edwin Drood, who die and are resurrected. Doubledick dies twice: once metaphorically, to his former life, when his sweetheart has said that 'Mary Marshall's lips' shall never address another word to him on earth. (When she speaks to him again it is, strangely enough, as another 'self', Mrs Richard Doubledick.) He joins the army and meets his better self, Captain Taunton, who tells him 'You are at the crisis of your fate' and exhorts him to 'retrieve his past'. Taunton is not only his guardian angel, but his witness. They become inseparable, and when Taunton dies Doubledick takes over his identity, in that he has become noble and courageous, and becomes a son to Taunton's mother. His second death (though of course like Manette and the others he is to rise from it) is surrounded by images of mortality:

> ... undisturbed by the moaning of men and the shrieking of horses ... ; dead, as to any sentient life that was in it, and yet

alive – the form that had been Lieutenant Richard Doubledick, with whose praises England rang, was conveyed to
Brussels. . . . Over and over again the sun rose and set upon
the crowded city; over and over again the moonlight nights
were quiet on the plains of Waterloo; and all that time was a
blank to what had been Lieutenant Richard Doubledick
. . . indifferent to all, a marble face lay on a bed, like the face
of a recumbent statue on the tomb of Lieutenant Richard
Doubledick.

Dickens is trying to convey to his readers that Doubledick is
dead, without actually saying so. In later books he is not so
scrupulous.

Our Mutual Friend opens with the finding of the apparent
corpse of John Harmon, the second chapter ends with the words
'Man's drowned!' and in chapter 3 the jury finds that the body of
Mr John Harmon 'had been discovered floating in the Thames,
in an advanced state of decay, and much injured.' Except for one
or two easily passed over hints, it is not until the thirteenth
chapter that we know definitely that John Harmon is alive. The
reader is also supposed to think that Eugene Wrayburn is dead,
when in chapter 6 of the fourth book the surgeon says, 'it is
much to be feared that she has set her heart upon the dead'. In
No Thoroughfare Marguerite, having saved her lover from
sinking into the glacier, holds 'both her loving hands upon the
heart that stood still', and in the next chapter Vendale is described as 'the unfortunate English gentleman who was killed on
the Simplon'. Dickens has at last found a way to express his
theme openly, when he is able to say: 'Vendale stood before his
murderer, a man risen from the dead.' And there is no doubt in
my mind that this situation would have appeared again in
Edwin Drood.

Both themes, of the split self and of the resurrection of the dead
appear next in *A Tale of Two Cities*, which came out in 1859. By
this time Dickens had gone through the upheavals and miseries
of falling in love with Ellen Ternan and separating from his wife;
it was perhaps the climax of his restless desperation. In a letter
to Forster about the separation he says, 'Quite dismiss from your
mind any reference whatever to present circumstances at home.
Nothing can put *them* right, until we are all dead and buried and
risen.'[3] The theme of 'putting things right' by being 'dead and

buried and risen' was, after its first statement in *The Story of Richard Doubledick*, to preoccupy him at intervals for the rest of his life. Indeed, *Buried Alive* was one of the titles he thought of for *A Tale of Two Cities*.

The inception of this book caused even more emotional upheaval than usual. 'Growing inclinations of a fitful and undefined sort are upon me sometimes to fall to work on a new book,' he wrote in January 1858. 'Then I think I had better not worry my worried mind yet awhile. Then I think it would be of no use if I did, for I couldn't settle to one occupation.'4 When he did in fact begin to work on it, he still had some difficulty: 'I cannot please myself with the opening of my story, and cannot in the least settle at it or take to it.'5

Dr Manette is Dickens' first attempt to bring two separate selves together in one character without the use of fantasy. His story opens with characteristic death-in-life imagery, in Mr Lorry's dream:

> He was on his way to dig someone out of a grave . . . A hundred times the dozing passenger inquired of this spectre:
> 'Buried how long?'
> The answer was always the same: 'Almost eighteen years.'
> 'You had abandoned all hope of being dug out?'
> 'Long ago.'
> 'You know that you are recalled to life?'
> 'They tell me so.'
> 'I hope you care to live?'
> 'I can't say.'

Lucie, on being told that her father is alive, says, 'I am going to see his Ghost! It will be his Ghost – not him!' And it is indeed a ghost that she sees: 'the task of recalling him from the vacancy into which he always sank when he had spoken, was like recalling some very weak person from a swoon, or endeavouring, in the hope of some disclosure, to stay the spirit of a fast-dying man'.

This ghost, this second self, has been created by wrong and suffering; the possibility of its return to take over the true self gives the Doctor 'a sudden sense of terror, like that which one may fancy strikes to the heart of a lost child'. The true self is restored by the ministrations of a woman who, though his daughter, is more like a mother to him. So far the character of Dr Manette is psychologically true to the theme that Dickens is trying to express – that the true self can be buried alive and yet be resurrected by maternal love – and as a literary device it is successful, when the doctor reverts to the second self in times of sorrow or disaster. By these means Dickens can forewarn us that Lucie's marriage holds the seeds of disaster, and can contrive that Darnay's rescue shall be undertaken by Carton alone. But as a means towards the unconscious analysis of his own psychology which I believe to be so strongly present in the later novels, the device is not so satisfactory. The two selves are not aware of each other, cannot communicate and therefore can never help or affect each other. This makes the situation both psychologically untrue and analytically sterile. So Dickens turns to Darnay and Carton, the divided self in two characters instead of one.

Darnay is Carton's true self: stable, courageous, loving, generous, able to apply all his faculties to good use, he is a fully developed personality. The two must resemble each other, not only for the devices of the plot, but because they are the same person. It is no accident that Carton is looking in a mirror when he says, 'There is nothing in you to like; you know that . . . A good reason for taking to a man, that he shows you what you have fallen away from, and what you might have been.' Darnay is indeed what Carton might have been; why Carton is not Darnay we are not told, but we know enough from Dickens' other characters with empty hearts, who have 'no business to be', to guess that he was never loved for what he was. There is nothing to like in him because those who should have found him lovable did not do so: he has conformed to their expectations of him. He hates Darnay, but finds in him his only means of salvation. By liberating the true self, the false self, though condemning itself to death, becomes for the first time what it might have been. Carton lives on, in the memory of those he has saved, as he was at his highest moment: as the true self he never could have been but for his death. Darnay, the true self, can not be saved: he *must* die, unless Carton dies in his place.

Carton naturally uses death-and-rebirth imagery when he talks about himself. He says to Lucie: 'I am like one who died young. All my life might have been.' He knows instinctively that the false self can never become the true self 'except it die'. Even his love for Lucie cannot save him: it kindled him into fire, but 'a fire, however, inseparable in its nature from myself, quickening nothing, doing no service, idly burning away'. The night before he changes places with Darnay in prison, the words of the burial service come into his mind again and again: 'I am the resurrection and the life ... he that believeth in me, though he were dead, yet shall he live ...'. Dickens seems uneasy about the repetition of these words all through the chapter and evidently feels he must produce some reason for it: 'the chain of association that brought the words home', he says, 'might have been easily found', but he does not tell us what that chain is. Still, whatever religious truth the words may hold, for Carton's situation they are psychologically exact.

Dickens seems to have been unconscious of what he was really writing about, because he propounded the life-in-death theme as an idea to be used in *Our Mutual Friend* as though it were completely new. 'I think,' he wrote, 'a man, young and perhaps eccentric, feigning to be dead, and *being* dead to all intents and purposes external to himself, and for years retaining the singular view of life and character so imparted, would be a good leading ingredient for a story.'[6] This may have been quite soon after the completion of *A Tale of Two Cities*, since Forster says that Dickens had chosen the title four years before its publication, and the above letter was written at some time between 1860 and 1864. At the beginning of this period Dickens wrote for the *New York Ledger* (and reprinted in *All the Year Round*) a potboiler called *Hunted Down*, supposed to be based on an incident in the life of Wainewright the poisoner. Either he was attracted to this incident because of its nature, or he was so obsessed by the theme of the two selves that he could not help introducing it into this short story. Meltham, the respectable young insurance agent thought to be dying for love of a dead girl, takes up a second life as Beckwith, 'the worst kind of drunkard very far advanced upon his shameful way to death'. He does this deliberately, to act as a spy upon and to bring to justice Slinkton the murderer. The story's only other interest is that it introduces the theme of the unknown watcher, which first occurs in *Martin Chuzzlewit* (in the character of Nadgett) and is later found in *Our Mutual Friend* (Riderhood), in *No Thoroughfare* (the lawyer Bintrey) and probably in *Edwin Drood* (Datchery).

Great Expectations leaves the theme of the two selves, to push the exploration of the search for the mother to its utmost limits. But *Our Mutual Friend* (1864) is full of death-and-rebirth plots and sub-plots: even a minor character like Rogue Riderhood is brought back from the dead. The first part of the novel opens with the finding of a body, supposedly that of John Harmon, followed by the arrival of Harmon himself to view his own body. There has been, in a way, a substitute death, a little like that of Carton for Darnay (except that Radfoot is not a willing victim). Radfoot and Harmon are not as much alike as Carton and Darnay, but are sufficiently alike to be mistaken for each other, and their lives have been remarkably similar. But Radfoot (the bad self) means to kill Harmon. The moment when Harmon realises this is comparable to the moment of psychological awareness experienced by someone previously uncertain of his own identity:

> I could not have said that my name was John Harmon – I could not have thought it – I didn't know it . . . I cannot possibly express it to myself without using the word I. But it is not I. There was no such thing as I, within my knowledge. It was only after a downward slide through something like a tube, and then a great noise and a sparkling and a crackling as of fires that the consciousness came upon me, 'This is John Harmon drowning! John Harmon, struggle for your life. John Harmon, call on heaven and save yourself!' I think I cried it out aloud in a great agony, and then a heavy horrid unintelligible something vanished, and it was I who was struggling alone in the water.

Now Dickens has brought about the situation he has been seeking ever since *The Story of Richard Doubledick*: Harmon is really alive, and yet he can say, 'it seemed as if the whole country were determined to have me dead. The Inquest declared me dead, the government proclaimed me dead: I could not listen at my fireside for five minutes to the outer world, but it was borne into my ears that I was dead.' But it is not John Harmon who still lives, it is John Rokesmith. Dickens calls him 'the living-dead man' and his task is to 'heap mounds upon mounds of earth over John Harmon's grave'. The self has split again and, as always, has enormous trouble in keeping the buried self under: 'still the sexton Rokesmith accumulated mountains over him, lightening his labour with the dirge, "Cover him, crush him, keep him down!" ' John Rokesmith also expresses 'with a gloomy brow' the wish that John Harmon had never been born; but he cannot be reborn until he has been accused and found innocent of murder – the murder of John Harmon. The scene in which three witnesses at the Harmon inquest are confronted with the living John Harmon is a forerunner of the scene in *No Thoroughfare* in which Vendale appears before Obenreizer, 'a man risen from the dead'; and, I am convinced, of a similar scene in *Edwin Drood*. In *Our Mutual Friend* the scene is over in a paragraph; but in *No Thoroughfare* it is something of a set piece, and in *Edwin Drood* it would probably (to judge from the cover illustration) have been the dénouement of the book.

Still, the Harmon–Rokesmith character is not really satisfactory for Dickens' purpose: it does not express the situation posed by his unconscious mind. The murdered self, Radfoot, had no part in Rokesmith's life; Rokesmith and Harmon are identical except in their manner of living, so that Rokesmith does not really bury his former self, only his former name. As soon as he marries Bella the split in his life is healed. So Dickens turns to the Wrayburn–Headstone situation, which comes much closer to the truth. Although in the novel their only point of contact is that they are both in love with Lizzie Hexam, Eugene Wrayburn and Bradley Headstone represent in fact parts of one personality – that of Dickens himself. It has already been observed that Dickens needed to confide in his readers, often under the thinnest veil of fiction, and it seems likely that this is what he is doing in *Our Mutual Friend*.

There is no evidence as to when Ellen Ternan became Dickens' mistress. Edgar Johnson puts the possible date as early as December 1862, without giving his reasons for doing so. But it seems to me more likely that it happened shortly before June 1865; perhaps the trip to Paris which occurred then was a honeymoon trip. At any rate Dickens attests that the manuscript account of Bella Wilfer's wedding day was with him in the railway carriage on the day of his return, so he was probably still at work on it or at least had written it not long before. It ends with a short but ecstatic epithalamium: 'And oh, there are days in this life worth life and worth death. And oh, what a bright old song it is, that oh, 'tis love, 'tis love that makes the world go round!' If as Wright says Ellen yielded reluctantly, or if as Edgar Johnson thinks the liaison did not – as of course it could not – fulfil Dickens' inner longings, it is probable that he would write so rapturously only in the first flush of possession.

If this is so, it means that while writing the larger part of *Our Mutual Friend* Dickens was what would then be called 'pursuing' Ellen Ternan. He was both Eugene Wrayburn and Bradley Headstone. Headstone's story continues Pip's story: both men are the prey of the same rending and irresistible compulsion. But Estella cannot love Pip because she cannot love; Lizzie can and does love – only she does not love Headstone. If it were merely that she loved Eugene more, Headstone's sorrow and bitterness might be borne, but she tells him that nothing could make her love him: 'I do not like you . . . I have never liked you from the first, and . . . no other living creature has anything to do with the effect you have produced upon me for yourself.'

Pip's situation is nearer to that of the rejected child, where the rejecting mother is too deprived or too immature to love; but Headstone's is nearer to the truth as the child experiences it – he feels himself not loved because of what he is. The child may construct another self which can be loved, but still the true self remains unloved and therefore, to the child, unlovable. This brings absolute despair, and Headstone expresses the child's desperate need when he says to Lizzie, 'It is I who should call for help . . . you don't know yet how much I need it', and 'you are the ruin – the ruin – the ruin – of me. I have no resources in myself, I have no confidence in myself, I have no government of myself when you are near me or in my thoughts.' It is precisely his self that lacks everything love might have given him. Dickens has reached the heart of his theme. It may be that the scene in which Headstone seems to be 'flinging his heart's blood down . . . in drops upon the paving-stones' really expresses the state of Dickens' own inner self: 'The wild energy of the man, now quite let loose, was absolutely terrible . . . "No man knows till the time comes what depths are within him. To some men it never comes; let them rest and be thankful! To me, you brought it; on me, you forced it; and the bottom of this raging sea," striking himself on the breast, "has been heaved up ever since." '

When the depths are heaved up, the monsters of the raging sea reveal themselves. Pip, whatever his faults, is seen as 'good';

Headstone, whatever his virtues, is finally 'bad'. The rejected child sees himself as bad simply because he is rejected: it seems to him that if he had been good he would have been loved. Dickens describes Headstone's compulsive love for Lizzie as sympathetically as he describes Pip's love for Estella. Headstone is blamed for nothing: he loves because he cannot help it, his love is what he is. 'It seemed to him as if all that he could suppress in himself he had suppressed, as if all that he could restrain in himself he had restrained, and the time had come – in a rush, in a moment – when the power of self-command had parted from him.' This is the authentic voice of feeling, and is more likely to have been evoked by Dickens' emotions after falling in love with Ellen (when his daughter described him as 'like a madman'[7]) than by Headstone's emotions after once meeting Lizzie for a short time. It is the buried self that is 'heaved up' from the 'raging sea', and when it comes to the surface it can only destroy the second self. From the moment that he is rejected, Headstone's sole object is to destroy Wrayburn.

Eugene Wrayburn, with his mannered flippancy, has been seen as a forerunner of the Wildean dandy; but his apparent shallowness and artificiality may come from Dickens' unconscious perception that he represents the second self, as Headstone's inability to restrain or conceal his emotions represents the inner self. Wrayburn also represents in some way Dickens' own conscious dilemma at this time. He too felt the compulsion of a love he could neither control nor abandon, a love which dominated him as it does Headstone, though in a different way. Ellen Ternan was of a fairly respectable family, enough of a lady to be accepted at Gad's Hill, but there was no possibility of Dickens' marrying her since he had no reason to divorce Catherine. So if Wrayburn's situation is to resemble his own, some reason must be contrived why it is impossible for him to marry Lizzie. In fact once this device has served its purpose Dickens evades the whole issue,* since Lizzie, though nominally a working girl, is a perfect lady with exquisite manners and good diction (even while she is illiterate) and

---

* As he evades the issue of Bella Wilfer's mercenary feelings, which are simply never tested, since she is never called on to undergo poverty with Rokesmith.

(once she has started work at the paper-mill) soft white hands. Why are her language and her manners so different from those of Pleasant Riderhood, another waterman's daughter? The answer is that Wrayburn could not possibly be attracted by a real working girl like Pleasant (although he has originally been attracted to Lizzie only by her beauty, knowing nothing of her manners or her character).

Dickens was at this time a respectable middle-aged novelist compulsively drawn to a young girl whom he could not marry. He must have been as bewildered by this as Wrayburn:

'Ah, Eugene,' said Lightwood affectionately, . . . 'I would that you answered my three questions! What is to come of it? What are you doing? Where are you going?'
'And, my dear Mortimer,' returned Eugene, . . . 'believe me, I would answer them instantly if I could. But to enable me to do so, I must first have found out the troublesome conundrum long abandoned. Here it is. Eugene Wrayburn. . . . Riddle-me, riddle-me-ree, perhaps you can't tell me what this may be? – No, upon my life I can't. I give it up!'

Dickens must often have asked himself the questions which Mortimer asks Eugene: 'Do you design to capture and desert this girl? . . . Do you design to marry her? . . . Do you design to pursue her?' Like Eugene, he answered no to the first two questions and probably, like him, came to the conclusion: 'Out of the question to marry her, and out of the question to leave her. The crisis!' It is at this point that the miracle happens for Eugene Wrayburn that did not happen for his creator. Bradley Headstone tries to murder him – in other words the buried self breaks out and tries to destroy the second self. In the novel Wrayburn cannot actually die and be resurrected, but all the imagery of death and rebirth is presented to show the new integrated self rising from the destruction of the second self. Wrayburn acquires all Headstone's passion and earnestness, while Headstone himself, representing what was bad in the true self, becomes irrelevant to Wrayburn's life and ultimately destroys himself.

Between *Our Mutual Friend* and *Edwin Drood* Dickens wrote the ghost story *The Signal-Man*, in which the man of the title is haunted by a Figure presaging disasters which the signalman can do nothing to avert. The final warning, equally unintelligible to him, is of his own death. The Figure stands at the entrance to a tunnel, near the 'danger-light', and sometimes shouts 'Look out! Look out!' This strange little story might be taken as an allegory of the dangers of repressing the true self (the signalman has, like Carton, misused his opportunities, 'gone down, and never risen again'). He works in a gloomy cutting like a 'great dungeon' which feels as though it were outside the 'natural world'. The Figure, the true self, is impelled to send unintelligible warnings of the disaster that must inevitably ensue.

But by the time Dickens came to write *Edwin Drood*, his entire concern was with double-self, life-in-death imagery. Jasper has a second, drug-induced personality; Helena is Neville's better self and is, as I think, to impersonate him as a living figure though he is dead; Edwin would return from the grave like Wrayburn as a true integrated self. But all this turns on the question of whether Edwin is really murdered or not.

One strange fact about the mystery has not, I think, been previously observed. This is that all the evidence that Edwin is dead comes from sources outside Dickens' own work: the evidence of the novel, studied within the pattern of Dickens' later works, shows the extreme likelihood of his being alive. Without the asseverations of Forster, Charles Dickens junior and Kate Perugini, the controversy could hardly have continued. Sir Luke Fildes' testimony is not of the same importance, since it shows no proof that Edwin is dead, only that Jasper attacked him with the intention of killing him – a fact that has never been in question. All these authorities have as their source purely oral tradition; and I shall try to show, first that this may be demolished or discounted, and then that the cumulative evidence of Dickens' own writings shows clearly that Edwin was not murdered.

Forster says that he first heard of the plan for *The Mystery of Edwin Drood* in a letter dated 6 August 1869: 'I . . . have a very curious and new idea for my new story. Not a communicable idea (or the interest of the book would be gone) but a very strong one, though difficult to work.' 'The story', Forster continues,' . . . was to be that of the murder of a nephew by his uncle; the originality of which was to consist in the review of the murderer's career by himself at the close . . . The last chapters were to be written in the condemned cell, to which his wickedness . . . had brought him.'[8] Now the value of his testimony rests on two things: Forster's accuracy and integrity in reporting, and the meaning of the word 'murder' as here used.

Concerning the first point, we know that Forster was in fact neither accurate nor honest as an editor: he played tricks with the transcription of Dickens' letters and he allowed all the deletions from *Edwin Drood* to be printed as part of the text without, in either case, a word to his readers. Kate Perugini, in her article in the *Pall Mall*, does not defend – nor indeed is she concerned with – Forster's honesty. She is solely concerned with her father's reputation:

> And so he told his plot to Mr Forster, as he had been accustomed to tell his plots for years past, and those who knew him must feel it impossible to believe that in this, the last year of his life, he should suddenly become underhand, we might say treacherous, to his old friend, by inventing for his private edification a plot that he had no intention of carrying into execution . . . My father was particularly careful never to wound the very sensitive nature of one who . . . had devoted his time and energy to making my father's path in life as smooth as so intricate a path could be made.[9]

We have here two statements: first that Dickens would not hurt Forster's feelings, and second that deceiving Forster would have involved inventing a different plot from that originally intended to be used. But neither of these statements is true. Dickens frequently quarreled with Forster, and had no objection to hurting his feelings. It is difficult to believe that Forster did not recognise his own portrait as Podsnap and that he was not hurt by it, yet Dickens not only felt no compunction, but wrote gleefully in a letter to his sister-in-law (just after the publication of the chapter called 'Podsnappery'): 'Forster fluttered about in the Atheneum . . . and pretended not to see me, but I saw in every hair of his whisker (left hand one) that he saw Nothing Else.'[10]

Mrs Perugini's contention that Dickens would be deceiving Forster if Edwin Drood had not in fact been murdered rests entirely on Forster's report: she has no evidence of her own to offer about the plot, and Forster does not quote Dickens' own words. Even if he was accurate in his reporting (and we know

that one of Podsnap's chief faults was to rely on his own
assumptions rather than listen to what was actually said) the use
of the word 'murder' does not always imply that the victim was
killed. As Chesterton says, 'Whenever anybody talks naturally
of the murder of a man whom the reader at least supposes to be
murdered, [the critics] draw the strict logical inference that the
victim could not possibly have escaped from the man who was
trying to murder him.'[11] In fact Dickens does use the word
'murderer' of Bradley Headstone, whose victim recovers; and in
No Thoroughfare he says that Vendale has been lost 'by a dreadful
death' when he is alive.

Forster seems to assume that Jasper must be in the condemned cell for the murder of Edwin; but he may well be there
for the murder of Neville Landless. So we see that even if Forster
is reporting accurately what he heard and not what he supposed
himself to have heard, Dickens' account of the plot does not
necessarily imply that Edwin is dead. In any case, Dickens
would not be likely to tell anyone whether he was dead or not,
since this was the very 'mystery' he was so anxious to preserve.
Chesterton again sums up the whole situation with his usual
acuteness:

> Forster himself reports Dickens as saying that he had con-
> ceived a new and original idea for that story . . . which must
> not be revealed beforehand, or the interest of the story would
> be gone. And yet, strangely enough, this is the very passage
> upon which many Dickensians base their insistence that the
> story *was* revealed beforehand; so that the interest of the
> story presumably *was* gone, even before the story was
> begun . . . But . . . they have cried aloud that we are calling
> Forster a liar or Dickens a hypocrite if we say there was an
> ambiguity. They regard Forster as infallible in everything
> except the one definite fact that he does definitely record; that
> Dickens refused to tell him the secret.[12]

Mrs Perugini merely upholds Forster's claim to know the
plot: she has no claim of her own that her father told her
anything about it. The single positive piece of evidence that
Edwin is dead comes from Charley Dickens, who said that he
asked his father, 'Of course Edwin Drood was murdered?' and
that Dickens replied, 'Of course. What else did you suppose?'[13]
Charley was remembering these words more than twenty years

after they were spoken, and we see that their whole force rests on the two small words 'of course'. Without those (and they might merely have been repeated quizzically as an echo) Dickens might have been asking what his son actually thought about the 'mystery'. Or, if he were capable of misleading his readers, why should he not have been capable of misleading his own son in order to enhance surprise at the dénouement? But if Charley's account is accurate, it is very remarkable that Dickens should reveal all to one member of his family (and that one not a particular favourite) and yet conceal the solution so carefully from all the other members of his household. Georgina Hogarth told Kate Perugini that she had asked Dickens, 'I hope you haven't really killed poor Edwin Drood?' to which he had replied, 'I call my book the Mystery, not the History, of Edwin Drood'[14] and that he would say nothing more. So we see that the whole weight of the evidence for Edwin's death rests on Charley's unsupported statement, recalled – or at least written down – many years after.

Sir Luke Fildes' testimony has always been accepted as evidence for Edwin's death, but it is no such thing. In a letter to *The Times* on 3 November 1905 he said that when he was preparing the illustrations for *Edwin Drood* Dickens had told him that Jasper must be drawn with a double neck-tie, 'for Jasper strangles Edwin Drood with it'. (In fact Dickens describes Jasper as wearing 'a large black scarf of strong close-woven silk, slung loosely round his neck'.) But nobody doubts that Jasper strangled Edwin; what we want to know is whether he strangled him long enough to kill him or only long enough to render him unconscious. Dickens might just as well have told the illustrators of other stories that Bradley Headstone must have an oar to batter Wrayburn with, or that Obenreizer must have a knife to stab Vendale; and yet neither of these victims dies. These statements of Dickens' contemporaries do not therefore establish beyond question the fact of Edwin's death. Dickens' own references suggest only that he is determined to keep the mystery intact. He specifically says to Forster that it is not a communicable idea, from which it is surely unreasonable to infer that he afterwards communicated it, as Forster claims. In a letter to James Fields, dated 14 January 1870, he wrote: 'at Nos. 5 and 6 the story will turn upon an interest suspended until the end.'

There is one more piece of 'external' evidence. In September 1869 a story called *John Acland*, by the Hon. Robert Lytton, was accepted for *All The Year Round*. It was about the murder of a man by his best friend, but since the body had been concealed under layers of ice, the crime could not be revealed until many months later. Now Richard Baker, in an article called *Who Was Dick Datchery?*, says that although Dickens refused to continue publication of this story on the grounds that the plot had been used previously, nevertheless 'he was himself to make use of a similar idea some six months later'.[15] But surely this is extremely unlikely? Dickens might have refused to take the story because it anticipated his own plot (for which the notes had already been made in August 1869) but he would hardly publish one instalment and then withdraw it from publication. It is far more likely that the plot of *Edwin Drood* did not in fact involve the discovery of a body.

In his own notes, dated 20 August 1869, Dickens lists seventeen possible titles for his new book. Several of them, notably *Flight and Pursuit, The Flight of Edwin Drood, Edwin Drood in Hiding* and *The Disappearance of Edwin Drood*, suggest at the very least that Dickens had not by that date made up his mind whether Edwin was to die or not, and so invalidate Forster's claim to know 'immediately after' 6 August[16] that Edwin was to be murdered. It is true that in subsequent notes Dickens does refer twice to the 'murder', but it is not impossible that an author, in making very brief notes solely for his own perusal, should write 'murder' rather than 'attempted murder'.

However, it is from the 'internal' evidence – that is, the evidence of Dickens' own writing – that I think it may be safe to presume Edwin to be alive. The resurrection of the supposed dead is a recurrent theme in his books, though in the early ones it is a fairly unimportant theme. Oliver Twist is not known by his aunt Rose Maylie to be living; Ralph Nickleby does not know that his son is alive; Barnaby Rudge's father, the murderer, has been alive all the years that he was thought to be dead; Marley returns (though as a ghost); in *The Cricket on the Hearth* Caleb Plummer's son, presumed dead, turns up to save the family fortunes; Trotty Veck thinks himself dead and allowed as a spirit to undergo penitential experiences; Captain Cuttle actually reads the burial service for Walter Gay, who later comes home alive and well. But in *Bleak House* this theme becomes part of the main plot: it is because Esther is alive, not dead as her mother supposed, that Guppy recognises her likeness to Lady Dedlock and thus enables Tulkinghorn to obtain the evidence he needs. In *A Tale of Two Cities* Dr Manette's resurrection both saves and destroys those he loves (and in a sub-plot Barsad's coffin is buried, while he himself is later discovered alive in Paris). In *A Message from the Sea* the young sailor Hugh Raybrock, presumed drowned, returns to clear his father's name of the stain of an imputed crime.

Our Mutual Friend contains two variants of this theme. In the first, John Harmon is attacked for his money and thrown into the Thames as dead; by chance the body of a man resembling him is fished out of the river and mistaken for him; he elects, for certain reasons, to remain dead. Eugene Wrayburn too is attacked and left for dead, and the reader is for some time in suspense as to whether he has died or will die. But it is *No Thoroughfare* which brings this theme to a head. Vendale is thought by the murderer *and by the reader* to be dead until the grand dénouement scene some three months after the attempted murder. Now this plot is so close to that of *Edwin Drood* (and, in one or two scenes, to that of *Our Mutual Friend*) that I cannot but think that Edwin, like Vendale, is alive and will bring about Jasper's downfall by returning from the dead – as indeed the bottom vignette in the cover design would appear to confirm. Of course it is possible that Dickens had worked through, and therefore was going to break away from, his obsession with the resurrected dead, but there is no sign that he is leaving this theme behind him.

In any case Bintrey, the lawyer and silent witness in *No Thoroughfare*, so closely resembles the lawyer Grewgious in *Edwin Drood* that it is likely they would play similar roles. Now why does Bintrey not accuse Obenreizer of murder as soon as he himself knows about it? The main reason is obviously that if he did the story would end there, and very tamely. How much better the dramatic confrontation of murderer and victim which actually takes place! But of course there must be an interior reason for the lapse of time; and doubtless it is the same reason in both stories. Vendale has to wait until he has recovered from his ordeal before he can confront Obenreizer; Edwin too would presumably take some time to get well, if his unconscious body has been thrown into the quicklime. Bintrey tells Obenreizer why they have waited so long to bring him to justice, in a speech which, it seems to me, might equally well be spoken by Grewgious to Jasper:

> I not only had no scruple in digging the pitfall under your feet in the dark – I felt a certain professional pleasure in fighting you with your own weapons. By my advice, the truth has been carefully concealed from you, up to this day. By my advice, the trap into which you have walked was set for you (you know why, now, as well as I do) in this place. There was but one certain way of shaking the devilish self-control which has hitherto made you a formidable man. That way has been tried, and (look at me as you may) that way has succeeded.

This speech could be even more dramatically appropriate to the circumstances of Jasper's exposure; I suppose the 'trap' to be Grewgious' having told him about the ring which Edwin (unknown to Jasper) was carrying in his pocket when attacked. Jasper would hurry to the lime-pit that night to remove this unsuspected evidence as to the identity of the body and, finding no trace of it there, would rush to the church tower where he had strangled Edwin, to see if it could be lying hidden there. As he rushes up the stairs we see the scene illustrated in the cover-picture: Edwin himself stands in the open doorway of the tower, a man returned from the dead, and at the bottom of the tower stair stands Helena, disguised as her twin brother Neville, whom Jasper really has murdered. This would be the most dramatic climax ever of a writer who loved and excelled in dramatic climaxes: the murderer trapped, as he thinks, between the ghosts of his two victims. It is a circumstance which might well shake the 'devilish self-control' which has hitherto made Jasper 'a formidable man'.

But Bintrey learned of the attempted murder from the victim, Vendale, himself. How has Grewgious learned about the attack on Edwin? It is obvious that he does know about it from his behaviour to Jasper on 26 December, when he has just told Jasper that Edwin and Rosa had broken off their engagement. Bintrey has formerly been on the friendliest terms with Jasper; he has remarked, 'I know your affection for your nephew, and that you are quick to feel on his behalf.' Why then does he, a naturally kindly man, offer no word of sympathy or comfort when

Jasper, apparently overwhelmed with grief at Edwin's disappearance, grovels on the floor in a fit or swoon? Why does he refuse to eat or drink with him? How does he know, as he evidently does, that Jasper has fainted not from grief but from the horror of having committed a wholly unnecessary crime? From whom could he have learned all this, if not from Edwin?

Edwin has been charged 'by the living and by the dead' to return Rosa's mother's ring to Grewgious, and this charge was evidently intended to form the basis of another scene of high melodrama, only to be revealed at the end of the book. The ring will be returned from the brink of the grave by a man both living and dead. This was to be *The Mystery of Edwin Drood*.

Conclusion

In his early books Dickens' plots and characters were mainly drawn from his observations, from his experiences as a journalist, from the countless melodramas he had seen, from the improving themes current in the moral climate of his time; all this bound together and seasoned with his own inimitable comic inventiveness. The themes which were to recur so constantly in the later books had not yet risen from the depths of his unconscious mind. We see hints of them like ripples on the surface, here and there: Oliver the orphan, Nancy the fallen woman, Nell's relationship to her grandfather as parent rather than as child, Nell's death. Sometimes certain episodes, such as the two 'buried-self' dreams in *Martin Chuzzlewit*, Jonas' fear of returning to himself and the return of the living dead in *Barnaby Rudge*, strike across the scene like single flashes of lightning. Dickens was occupied in constructing that impregnable outer self that should assure his personal, social and literary future. With *Pickwick Papers, Oliver Twist* and *Nicholas Nickleby* he had consolidated his reputation as a novelist, *The Old Curiosity Shop* had brought him a kind of fame never before given to a novelist, and his tour of America in 1842 showed him that he attracted even more interest there than in England. And then things began to go wrong.

America fell short of his dreams: although he was flattered and fêted everywhere, he was sickened by slavery and repelled by the primitive lack of hygiene. As the tour went on, he became more and more outspoken about the things he disliked: 'I don't like the country,' he wrote to Forster, 'I would not live here, on any consideration.'[1] The last days of the visit were soured by the reaction of American publishers to the memorial on copyright, signed by himself and other well-known English writers, published in the New York *Evening Post*. Besides this, a forged letter purporting to be written by Dickens himself and strongly abusive of American manners and morals appeared in the New York papers after his departure, and was received with rage and vituperations against him all over the country.

At home, he felt that his novels were enriching everyone but himself; and indeed Macrone, Chapman and Hall, Bentley and a crowd of literary pirates were all making as much as or more than he was himself. When he tried to take legal proceedings against some of the latter, it cost him seven hundred pounds, and within a year or two the pirates were back at their profitable tricks. The sales of *Martin Chuzzlewit* were disappointing, though he felt it to be his best book yet; and in spite of what Forster calls 'the prodigious immediate success' of *A Christmas Carol*, the profits from it were much less than Dickens had hoped for, less than he needed to discharge 'terrific' debts,[2] and this was undoubtedly due to thoughtlessness on the part of his publishers, with whom he broke off relations. 1843 had been, says Forster, 'a year of much anxiety and strange disappointments'[3] and it is possible that Dickens, 'famous, happy and caressed', now began to feel again those sensations of pain and resentment at the neglect of those whose business it was to look after his interests, which he described himself to have experienced when his parents, as it seemed to him, abandoned any kind of care for him.

These feelings may have been sharpened by his loneliness when he found himself in Italy in 1844, far from his friends, his home and the familiar London streets. No doubt the anxiety and depression to which he refers in his letters had greater depths beneath, which he suppressed even from his own knowledge. Whatever the reasons, the themes which were henceforth to play their parts in every succeeding book now began to reveal themselves.

The Chimes (1844) first discusses the question of the right to be born, later to recur in *Dombey, Bleak House* and *A Tale of Two Cities*, as well as in some of the short stories; it wore itself out, apparently, in the first part of *Great Expectations*, but started up again in *George Silverman's Explanation* (1868) with a desperate force which shows it to be one of the themes that was never worked through. *Dombey and Son*, begun in 1846, begins to explore themes which had earlier appeared in undeveloped forms: the death of the child, the empty heart, and in Florence herself the unloved child who has no right to be born. Dickens' sustained study of this subject, which holds the key to all the other themes, may have been what suggested the writing of the autobiographical fragment at about this time – it was first thought of after the mention of Mrs Pipchin in the third number of *Dombey* had brought back memories of his factory days.

The Haunted Man (1847) rejects the idea that oblivion of 'early sorrow and wrong' may wipe out the misery arising from it. (This must, however unconscious itself, have been taken by the unconscious mind as encouragement to go on sending up more memories!) The Haunted Man himself reappears as an almost identical character in *Mugby Junction* (1866), also seeking oblivion of early unhappiness, this time in the form of running away from his birthday (the day of his birth). *David Copperfield* (1849–50) makes use of all the conscious memories of the traumatic period and these bring up the unconscious ones of the search for the mother, betrayal by the parent and (indirectly) the right to be born. This becomes the main theme of *Bleak House*, and Lady Dedlock carries on the theme of the empty heart, as Louisa does in *Hard Times* (1854) and Clennam and Miss Wade do in *Little Dorrit* (1855–57). *A Tale of Two Cities* (1859) takes up the life-in-death theme and the idea of the split self, both later to be fully explored in *Our Mutual Friend* (1864–65) and *Edwin Drood* (1870). *Great Expectations* brings to a close one aspect of the search for the mother (though another aspect is brought up in *Our Mutual Friend* and *Edwin Drood*) and seems to dispose of the theme of the empty heart.

It may be argued that to see these themes and characters as having their source in Dickens' unconscious mind is to make his writings into casebooks of psychology rather than great creative works. But there is no reason why, in accepting the unconscious level, we should lose what Dickens has been to many generations of readers. His marvellously inventive prose, his acute perception, his unrivalled comic genius will be what they always were; but we may expect new insights into what seemed obscure and new dimensions in what seemed commonplace, while what formerly seemed relevant only to the Victorian age will be found to have permanent value (not as social, but as human commentary). To give a single example: most critics agree in saying that Dickens never creates a real woman, but if this is so it is extremely unlikely that so great a genius will be merely doing less well what other writers can do better; it behoves the critics to find out what Dickens is really doing (whether consciously or unconsciously) in creating these apparently defective characters. To accept a critical statement about an author which does not fit in with the rest of what one knows about him is to insult him with a shallow understanding and an inaccurate judgment.

To discuss, or even to present, social or metaphysical questions with any degree of impartiality is only possible to a human being who has in some sense come to terms with his own psychology: if he has not, all kinds of unconscious motivations will affect not only his judgment but also how he actually sees the question. We must know ourselves before we can truly know others or fully recognise their rights and their relationships. George Eliot is a writer of this kind: she can write about the human soul in its many uncertainties, emotional, moral or religious, because she knows herself. Dickens cannot write about the soul because he does not yet know about the self; it is the exploration of the self that concerns him in his books, not the exploration of social problems. His solutions to these are all purely emotional, as are his responses to them. He may comment on the social conditions of his times, but he is incapable of an impartial view of any of them because of his own powerful unconscious motivations.

But when those drives and the feelings that arise from them are what he is writing about, then he is the Master; no other novelist, not even Dostoyevsky, writes with such penetrating intensity about the sorrows of the empty heart. Many critics have regarded Dickens as a caricaturist, but this is merely a defective description, arising from an imperfect understanding, of the very quality of his imagination. Emotionally he remained undeveloped and so he saw people as a child sees them, unchanging and recognisable by certain immutable characteristics. Those of us who have a vivid remembrance of our own early days know how accurate this vision can be. But there may be another reason why the charge of caricature should so often be made.

Dickens aimed at making all his characters naturalistic; he thought he had succeeded in this aim, and hotly defended himself against criticism which dared to question his success. But in fact wherever his characters intersect, as it were, those themes which arise from his unconscious motivations, they become not myth, not allegory, but a something which is neither and yet pertains to both. The human heart feels intensely, but except in severe emotional disturbance its feelings are qualified and affected by other simultaneous emotions. But Dickens' characters seem, when the mythic light shines over them, only to feel one overwhelming emotion: they stand as signposts in the country of the heart. Edith Dombey is a paradigm of what happens when the heart bursting with one intense feeling, her resentment, is rent by another equally intense, her love for Florence. In her struggles, her tortures and her final abandonment to hatred, no other feeling can exist. Miss Wade has no life but the indulgence of her bitter resentment against Gowan and against life: love itself is in her only a form of the dominant emotion. Estella reveals the final paradox of a heart so full of rending emotions that it is empty of anything that can make it human.

Mythopoeic literature may be difficult to write, but it is not impossible. Spenser often does it successfully, Shakespeare does it in *The Winter's Tale* and *The Tempest*, George Macdonald can sometimes do it. But to combine naturalistic and mythopoeic writing is impossible – only, when a genius attempts it, his failure may be more significant than success in other modes. Still, the mere attempt to combine the two forms causes shifts and dislocations that may fill the uncomprehending reader with unease. But to regard Dickens' work as merely naturalistic is to lay it open to the most perverse misjudgments and, if these are persisted in, to actual misreadings of the text in attempts to force it into a genre not its own. Plot has, or should have, a secondary significance in mythopoeic writing; it is what the characters are, not what they do, that is important. Edith Dombey's years of exile with Cousin Feenix are not so much necessary to the plot as essential to the symbolic content, like Helena's years in the house of Paulina in *The Winter's Tale*. Mr Meagles' cottage is in the realistic mode; Miss Wade's house in Calais is in the symbolic, as is shown by Dickens' change of style: the words 'the shrubs that were dead, and the fountain that was dry, and the statue that was gone' are repeated like a refrain at the end of certain passages. Within every one of Dickens' books is a second story, which tells the saga of the heart.

'It is the great novelists above all who give us our social history,' F. R. Leavis has said; 'compared with what is done in *their* work – their creative work – the histories of the professional social historian seem empty and unenlightened.' Perhaps; but to value a novelist because he is a social historian may lead – and I think in some English departments has led – to his being valued only, or primarily, as a historian and hardly at all as a novelist. For any unbiased observer may give us an account of social or historical conditions, but only the artist can show us the life of the heart. The psychologist and the psychiatrist can report the results of their experiments and their observations, the novelist and the poet reveal the human predicament to us from within. It is not that Dickens is an expert in the geography of the heart; but one country, one landscape, he knows intimately and intensely. Like Proust, he heard throughout his life the sobs which had shaken him as a child. He has been valued as a novelist for many unrivalled qualities; he should be valued for this too.

John Carey sees Dickens as 'essentially a comic writer',[4] but it would be true to say that he is as essentially a tragic writer, since in all but a few of his books he shows us what it feels like to be, or to have been, a child who can never find what it has never been given, its birthright of love. He has illuminated for us the sufferings of the empty heart, but it is from his own heart that the light streams. Forster, for all his long friendship with Dickens, was not always particularly sensitive to the most profound connections between the life and the writings; but he was not mistaken when he said that 'Dickens's childish sufferings, and the sense they burnt into him of the misery of loneliness and a craving for joys of home, though they led to what was weakest in him, led also to what was greatest.'[5]

Notes and References

The following abbreviations have been used:

Life   John Forster, *The Life of Charles Dickens* (London, 1872–74).
CDTT   Edgar Johnson, *Charles Dickens, His Tragedy and Triumph* (New York, 1977).
DD   Gladys Storey, *Dickens and Daughter* (London, 1939).
WCD   Angus Wilson, *The World of Charles Dickens* (London, 1970).
LCD   Thomas Wright, *The Life of Charles Dickens* (London, 1935).

For readers using early editions of Forster's *Life*, I have included page numbers for greater ease of identification of references. Dates of letters in brackets indicate attribution; a question mark indicates uncertainty.

INTRODUCTION

1. C. S. Lewis, 'Edmund Spenser, 1552–99', in *Studies in Mediaeval and Renaissance Literature*, p. 143.
2. Philip Collins, *Dickens and Crime*, p. 17, p. 25 et passim. See especially p. 319: 'His change of mind on some important issues . . . has passed unnoticed.'
3. John Carey, *The Violent Effigy*, ch. 1.
4. *Life*, vol. III, ch. 9, p. 203.

CHAPTER 1

1. Emily Brönte, *Poems by Emily Brontë*, ed. A. C. Benson, poem no. 135.
2. Jules Henry, 'The Dialect of Nothingness', in *Pathways to Madness*, p. 110.
3. Bruno Bettelheim, 'Marcia: Extending the Self', in *The Empty Fortress*.
4. Karen Horney, 'Alienation from Self', in *Neurosis and Human Growth*. But see also 'The Search for Glory'.
5. *Life*, vol. I, ch. 3, p. 52.
6. George Dolby, *Charles Dickens as I Knew Him*, p. 30.
7. To Angela Burdett Coutts, 12/2/1864.
8. To Mark Lemon, 26/4/1855.
9. W. C. Macready, *Diaries*, 27/12/1845.
10. Edmund Yates, *Edmund Yates, His Recollections and Experiences*, vol. II, p. 94.
11. Eliza Lynn Linton, *My Literary Life*, pt II, p. 61.
12. *Life*, vol. III, ch. 7, p. 175.
13. Ibid., ch. 10, p. 214.
14. Ibid., ch. 7, p. 164.
15. To Angela Burdett Coutts, 18/3/1845.

16. H. C. Dent, *The Life and Characters of Charles Dickens*, ch. 12. This was early in 1856.
17. To Forster (August 1851).
18. To Mrs Watson, 7/12/1857.
19. To Edward Bulwer-Lytton, 5/1/1851.
20. *Life*, vol. III, ch. 7, p. 158.
21. To Forster (11/10/1846).
22. To Forster, 5/9/1857.
23. To Forster, 1/10/1858.
24. To Mary Dickens, 23/11/1861.
25. To Mary Dickens, 1/2/1863.
26. To Forster (June 1862).
27. Henri Taine, *History of English Literature*, trans. H. van Laun, bk V, ch. 1, p. 341.
28. Ibid., p. 344.
29. G. H. Lewes, 'Dickens in Relation to Criticism', in *Fortnightly Review*, February 1872.
30. *Life*, vol. III, ch. 14, p. 302 footnote.
31. To Mary Boyle, 8/5/1852.
32. To Forster (April 1856).
33. To Forster (October 1857).
34. Graham Greene, 'The Young Dickens', in *The Lost Childhood and Other Essays*, pp. 51–57.
35. G. K. Chesterton, *Charles Dickens*, p. 122.
36. *Life*, vol. I, ch. 2, p. 33.

CHAPTER 2

1. *Life*, vol. I, ch. 2, p. 49.
2. Ibid., p. 31.
3. Ibid., p. 31.
4. Ibid., p. 35.
5. Ibid., p. 37.
6. Ibid., p. 35.
7. *CDTT*, vol. I, pt I, ch. 3, p. 33.
8. *Life*, vol. I, ch. 1, p. 18.
9. Ibid., ch. 2, pp. 38–39.
10. To John Overs, 8/8/1841.
11. *Life*, vol. II, ch. 20, p. 458.
12. Ibid., vol. I, ch. 1, p. 6.
13. Ibid., ch. 2, p. 45.
14. Ibid., p. 50.
15. To Forster (11/8/1839).
16. To Maria Beadnell, 19/5/1833.
17. To T. J. Thompson, 28/2/(1844).
18. To T. J. Thompson, 11/3/1844.
19. Ibid.

20. He later came to recognise this trait in himself. See letter to Mrs Watson, 7/12/1857: 'I don't like the Realities except when they are unattainable – *then*, I like them of all things.'
21. To Thomas Mitton, 30/8/1846.
22. To Emile de la Rue, 17/8/1846.
23. To Maria Beadnell, 18/3/(1833).
24. To Catherine Hogarth (late May 1835).
25. To Thomas Beard (17/5/1837).
26. *Life*, vol. I, ch. 6, p. 98.
27. *LCD*, pts 40 and 115.
28. Ibid., pt 40.
29. To Catherine Hogarth (June 1835).
30. To George Thomson, 8/5/1837. Dickens used the same phrase in four other letters, and 'the grace and ornament' to George Cox (8/5/1837).
31. To Harrison Ainsworth (17/5/1837).
32. To Richard Johns (31/5/1837).
33. To Edward Chapman (7/5/1837). To Thomas Beard (17/5/1837) he added: 'The very last words she whispered were of me.'
34. To Forster (October 1837).
35. To Richard Lane, 2/1/1844.
36. To T. J. Thompson, 17/10/1845.
37. *Life*, vol. III, ch. 1, p. 12.
38. F. R. & Q. D. Leavis, *Dickens the Novelist*, p. 51.
39. To Maria Winter, 15/2/1855.
40. F. R. & Q. D. Leavis, *Dickens the Novelist*, p. 51.
41. Ibid., p. 52.
42. To Forster (April 1856).
43. Ibid.
44. To Forster (January 1855).
45. To Forster (October 1854).
46. *Life* gives March 1858, but correct date must be after Dickens' return from Edinburgh on 26/3/1858.
47. To Forster, ?/10/1857.

CHAPTER 3

1. F. R. & Q. D. Leavis, *Dickens the Novelist*, p. 54.
2. Ibid.
3. To George Dolby, 25/9/1869.
4. To Mrs Gore, 27/9/1852.
5. *CDTT*, vol. II, pt 8, ch. 3, p. 991.
6. To Forster (October 1860).
7. *DD*, p. 93.
8. *CDTT*, vol. II, pt 8, ch. 3, p. 991.
9. Ibid.
10. *WCD*, ch. 6, p. 271.

CHAPTER 4

1. *WCD*, ch. 2, p. 59.
2. To Angela Burdett Coutts, 9/10/1851.
3. *WCD*, ch. 6, p. 271.
4. Alfred T. Dickens, 'My Father and his Friends', in *Nash's Magazine*, September 1911.
5. *CDTT*, vol. II, pt 8, ch. 1, p. 752.
6. *Life*, vol. III, ch. 7, p. 153 et seq.
7. To Forster (October 1864).
8. *Life*, vol. III, ch. 7, p. 157.
9. Ibid.
10. To Forster (April 1856).

CHAPTER 5

1. To Angela Burdett Coutts, 16/3/1852.
2. *Life*, vol. II, ch. 1, p. 13.
3. Ibid., vol. I, ch. 9, p. 145.
4. Una Pope-Hennessy, *Charles Dickens, 1812–1870*, ch. 19, p. 294.
5. To Maria Winter, 22/2/1855.
6. 'The Ruffian', in *The Uncommercial Traveller*.
7. To Angela Burdett Coutts, 16/9/1843.
8. *Life*, vol. I, ch. 3, pp. 53–4.
9. To Mrs Brown, 5/7/1856.
10. *DD*, p. 96.
11. Mary Dickens, *Charles Dickens by his Eldest Daughter*, bk III, p. 64.
12. To Forster (8/1/1841).
13. To Samuel Williams (31/3/1840).
14. To Forster (?8/3/1840).
15. *Life*, vol. II, ch. 6, p. 126.
16. To George Cattermole, 14/1/(1841).
17. To Forster (3/11/1840).
18. To Angela Burdett Coutts, 18/1/1847.
19. To Forster (3/10/1846).
20. To Forster (6/12/1846).
21. To Forster, 20/8/1850.

CHAPTER 6

1. *CDTT* gives *Life*, ed. and annotated by J. W. T. Ley (1928), ch. 6, p. 19, n. 15.
2. To Forster, 2/22/1844.
3. To Forster, 2/11/1844.
4. *Life*, vol. III, ch. 6, pp. 138–139.
5. Ibid., ch. 14, p. 326.
6. Hugh Kingsmill, *The Sentimental Journey*, ch. 1, p. 2.
7. To W. H. Wills, 28/6/1867.

CHAPTER 7

1. Julian Moynihan, 'The Hero's Quest: The Case for Great Expectations', in *Essays in Criticism*, January 1960.
2. H. Daleski, *Dickens and the Art of Analogy*, pp. 242–243.
3. To Forster, who dates it March 1858, but *CDTT* dates it early April.
4. To Forster, 27/1/1858.
5. To Forster, 21/2/1858.
6. To Forster (10/1/1860).
7. *DD*, p. 96.
8. *Life*, vol. III, ch. 18, p. 425.
9. Kate Perugini, 'Edwin Drood and the Last Days of Charles Dickens', in *Pall Mall Magazine*, June 1906.
10. To Georgina Hogarth, 28/7/1864.
11. G. K. Chesterton, Introduction to *Edwin Drood* in the Everyman Library (1909).
12. Ibid.
13. Charles Dickens Jr., Introduction to *Edwin Drood* (1931).
14. Kate Perugini, 'Edwin Drood and the Last Days of Charles Dickens', in *Pall Mall Magazine*, June 1906.
15. Richard Baker, 'Who was Dick Datchery?' in *The Drood Murder Case*.
16. *Life*, vol III, ch. 18, p. 425.

CONCLUSION

1. To Forster (15/3/1842).
2. To Forster, 10/2/1844.
3. *Life*, Vol II, ch. 2, p. 39.
4. John Carey, *The Violent Effigy*, Introduction.
5. *Life*, vol. III, ch. 19, p. 473.

Select Bibliography

I have used the Oxford University Press edition of the works of Charles Dickens, published as *The Oxford Illustrated Dickens*. I have also used the Nonesuch Edition of *The Letters of Charles Dickens*, edited by Walter Dexter (London, 1938) and the Pilgrim Edition of *The Letters of Charles Dickens*, edited by Madeline House, Graham Storey and Kathleen Tillotson (Oxford, 1965, 1969, 1974, 1977).

Aylmer, Felix, *The Drood Case* (London, 1964).
Aylmer, Felix, *Dickens Incognito* (London, 1959).
Carey, John, *The Violent Effigy: A Study of Dickens' Imagination* (London, 1973).
Chesterton, G. K., *Charles Dickens* (London, 1906).
Chesterton, G. K., *The Victorian Age in Literature* (London, 1913).
Collins, Philip, *Dickens and Crime* (London, 1963).
Collins, Philip, *Dickens and Education* (London, 1962).
Daleski, H., *Dickens and the Art of Analogy* (London, 1970).
Dent, H. C., *The Life and Characters of Charles Dickens* (London, n.d.).
Dickens, Mary, *Charles Dickens by his Eldest Daughter* (London, 1910).
Dolby, George, *Charles Dickens as I Knew Him: The Story of the Reading Tours in Great Britain and America (1866–1870)* (London, 1912).
Forster, John, *The Life of Charles Dickens* (London, 1872–1874).
Forsyte, Charles, *The Decoding of Edwin Drood* (London, 1980).
Greene, Graham, *The Lost Childhood and Other Essays* (London, 1951).
Johnson, Edgar, *Charles Dickens, His Tragedy and Triumph* (New York, 1977).
Kingsmill, Hugh, *The Sentimental Journey* (London, 1934).
Leavis, F. R. & Q. D., *Dickens the Novelist* (London, 1970).
Lewes, G. H., *Literary Criticism of George Henry Lewes*, ed. A. R. Kaminsky (London, 1964).
Linton, Eliza Lynn, *My Literary Life* (London, 1899).
Macready, W. C., *The Diaries of William Charles Macready*, ed. W. Toynbee (London, 1912).
Pope-Hennessy, Una, *Charles Dickens, 1812–1870* (London, 1945).
Storey, Gladys, *Dickens and Daughter* (London, 1939).
Taine, Henri, *History of English Literature*, trans. H. van Laun (Edinburgh, 1871).
Watt, George, *The Fallen Woman in the Nineteenth Century Novel* (London, 1984).
Wilson, Angus, *The World of Charles Dickens* (London, 1970).
Wright, Thomas, *The Life of Charles Dickens* (London, 1935).

Psychological studies

Bettelheim, Bruno, *Love is not Enough* (London, 1952).

Bettelheim, Bruno, *The Empty Fortress* (New York, 1967).
Henry, Jules, *Pathways to Madness* (New York, 1972).
Horney, Karen, *The Neurotic Personality* (London, 1937).
Horney, Karen, *Neurosis and Human Growth* (London, 1951).

General Index

Index of Works and Characters